BAD EDUCATION

www.penguin.co.uk

Also by Matt Goodwin

Values, Voice and Virtue
National Populism
Revolt on the Right

Bad Education

Why Our Universities Are Broken
and How We Can Fix Them

MATT GOODWIN

bantam

TRANSWORLD PUBLISHERS
Penguin Random House, One Embassy Gardens,
8 Viaduct Gardens, London sw11 7bw
www.penguin.co.uk

Transworld is part of the Penguin Random House group of companies
whose addresses can be found at global.penguinrandomhouse.com

Penguin
Random House
UK

First published in Great Britain in 2025 by Bantam
an imprint of Transworld Publishers

A CIP catalogue record for this book
is available from the British Library.

ISBN
9781787635241

Text design by Couper Street Type Co.
Typeset in 11.75/16pt Granjon LT Std by Jouve (UK), Milton Keynes.
Printed and bound in Great Britain by Clays Ltd, Elcograf S.p.A.

The authorized representative in the EEA is Penguin Random House Ireland,
Morrison Chambers, 32 Nassau Street, Dublin D02 YH68.

This book is dedicated to the many students I have taught in the past and the many more who will follow in the future, with the hope that our universities will better serve the next generation.

Contents

Why I Decided to Speak Out

Somebody once said working in a university is one of the few places where you get older while everyone around you stays the same age.

I think about that every September, at the start of a new academic year, when another load of first-year students descend on to campus with hopes and dreams of receiving a world-class university education.

I used to be enthusiastic about their arrival. I used to welcome them with open arms. I used to tell them, excitedly, that they were about to embark on the intellectual adventure of their young lives. I used to wax lyrical about how they were setting out on a search for all the things universities are meant to protect and promote – knowledge, wisdom, evidence, reason and, above all, truth.

And much like the record numbers of students who are now heading off to university each year, many of them supported by the Bank of Mum and Dad, I used to believe that our universities would teach them the importance of debating in good faith, respecting alternative viewpoints, and prioritizing evidence over dogma.

But that was a long time ago.

In more recent years, instead, I found myself experiencing very different feelings. As each cohort of first-year students came and went, I found myself becoming more disillusioned, more disgruntled, more dispirited, more depressed.

Why?

Because after devoting more than twenty years of my life to universities – to teaching students, carrying out research, and helping run these increasingly complex and sprawling institutions – I've become aware of something many other professors know to be true but will simply never say out loud.

Our universities are broken.

They are completely and utterly broken. They are no longer fit for purpose. They have lost sight of their original mission. And they are now setting up an entire generation of young people to fail, weakening our society and democracy along the way.

The crisis that is now engulfing universities across the West, as we will see in the pages to come, has been decades in the making. It is a crisis very few university insiders are willing to talk about openly, directly and honestly, and which my fellow professors will be furious with me for writing about so candidly.

You see, there's a sort of secret code of silence among professors and academics on campus – what the Mafia call *omertà*. No matter how bad things get, no matter how glaringly obvious the crisis becomes, no matter how visibly these once great institutions are failing our young people, you just never, ever tell people on the outside.

Well, to hell with that. I'm going to tell you everything. I'm going to pull back the curtain, lift the lid, and show you why our universities are falling apart, and how this crisis is now trickling out of the universities to weaken our wider society – our politics, culture, institutions and ways of life. I'm going to explain exactly why we're letting down not only the millions of students who are passing through these institutions each year but also their families who are having to fork out increasingly astronomical sums of money to bankroll this experience. And I'm going to show you how the crisis on campus is unfolding in three key areas: how it's impacted the *scholars* who are supposed to be able to teach and conduct research with complete freedom; how it's undermining *students*, who are supposed to be able to study, learn and express themselves freely without having to fear the consequences; and how the surrounding *system* of higher education, which is supposed to guide and support our universities, is being corrupted.

I'm also going to propose some *solutions*, give you a

roadmap for fighting back, a clear set of ideas for how we can tackle this crisis and return universities to what they used to be – world-leading institutions of higher education that were committed to the pursuit of truth and learning, and were not afraid to expose our young people to the full range of ideas and opinions that exist in wider society, even ones they find uncomfortable.

And I'm going to do this because I genuinely care about these institutions. I have been writing this book in secret for a long time precisely because I *do* want to help save the universities and because I believe that our children, the next generation of leaders, thinkers and creators, deserve so much better.

And the only way to do that, the only way to build something better, is to step back to make full sense of the crisis that is now sitting, like a ticking time bomb, at the very heart of these institutions.

So, this is why I decided to blow up my career as a professor. This book is a shot across the bows of the establishment and a threat to the established order of things. Put simply, after reading this, it is highly likely that the established universities will never hire me and my former academic colleagues will never speak to me again.

Perhaps then, reader, you would consider doing me one favour. I don't expect you to agree with every-thing in the pages ahead, and I don't expect you to agree with my own views and opinions. They are just that, strongly held views and sometimes controversial opinions. But they are always based on facts, including studies and publicly reported cases, as the references in the Notes demonstrate. This is to enable you to decide for yourself. But what I do hope you will agree with me about is the need to crack open a much wider conversation about what is going wrong on campus and how we might fix it.

As we will see, while we claim to live in liberal, open societies, the blunt reality is that we are becoming less willing to tolerate different viewpoints and perspectives. That needs to change, especially in the very institutions that are supposed to be training and encouraging our young people to do exactly this.

Because if nothing else, those young people, our students, our leaders of tomorrow, will shape the future. They deserve a lot more than the broken status quo.

Matt Goodwin
October 2024

I

What Happened to You?

In 2024, after more than twenty years teaching and working in the universities, I quit my job as a university professor.

Most of my friends, family and colleagues thought I had gone completely insane. My mother has still not forgiven me. She liked telling the neighbours her son was a professor. How could you leave one of the best jobs on the planet, they asked? A job that comes with a generous salary, an even more generous pension, loads of autonomy, and the opportunity to travel the world and shape the bright young minds of tomorrow?

It's a good question. And to be honest it's one I never thought I'd have to answer. When I first entered the universities, in the early 2000s, during the big expansion of higher education under Tony Blair and New Labour, I fell completely in love with university life. I was a true believer. I believed passionately in what I thought universities and higher education were all about. The search for truth. The pursuit of knowledge.

Rigorously testing new ideas and expanding our understanding of the world. Fostering open, inquisitive discussion and debate among our students. And defending things like free speech and free expression, the lifeblood of liberal democracy.

Universities weren't always like this, of course. When they first emerged, nearly 1,000 years ago, in places like Bologna, Paris, Oxford, Cambridge and St Andrews in Scotland, many of them were openly religious institutions guided by people of faith, and strictly followed the rigid orthodoxy of the day.[1] In their early days universities were organized around only a small number of true believers, sacred values that could never be questioned, and a culture that was deeply intolerant of any dissenters.

But, as historian Niall Ferguson points out, from the nineteenth century onwards universities gradually became more secular and professional. So much so that by the twentieth century there had emerged a general agreement that their main purpose was not to pursue religious dogma but, instead, truth, which would be discovered through means such as freedom of conscience, thought, speech and publication.[2] This is why, even today, the world's elite universities, such as Harvard and Yale, still have 'veritas', or 'truth', as their guiding motto.

There was also agreement about other things, too. There would be no discrimination when admitting students or selecting people for academic jobs, other than on the basis of intellectual merit. And aside from having 'tenured' jobs, which basically meant they could not be sacked, university academics and professors would also be protected by something called 'academic freedom' – the freedom to research, write and say whatever they liked without fear of consequence, such as being harassed or fired for their views.

This was crucial. Because without academic freedom, university professors would simply never be able to test new but unfashionable ideas, challenge a prevailing groupthink that might be popular but also misleading, and push knowledge forward.

This also helps to explain why, even today, universities are still often referred to as Ivory Towers, which in the Christian tradition is a symbol of noble purity. The Ivory Tower is a metaphorical place where scholars and students can cut themselves off from the outside world and feel free to pursue their interests without fearing consequences.

And it really worked. By championing truth and objective scientific knowledge, and debating in good faith, universities in the West helped produce one of the greatest civilizations the world has ever seen.

Even today, all but one of the top ten universities in the world and nearly three-quarters of the top hundred are based in the West. Without these institutions it is difficult if not impossible to imagine things such as the post-war economic boom, the triumph of liberal democracy over fascism and communism, and countless scientific discoveries from the internet to vaccines taking place.[3]

And all this is pretty much what I thought I was joining when I decided, after finishing my undergraduate degree, to stay on campus and devote the rest of my life to becoming an academic.

I thought I was joining institutions that prioritized scientific knowledge, evidence and reason over religious and political dogma. I thought I was joining institutions that were genuinely committed to helping students become critical, well-rounded thinkers by exposing them to a wide range of ideas, even ones they profoundly disagreed with and might even find uncomfortable.

As John Stuart Mill argued in his book *On Liberty*, freedom of speech can only flourish if you have a genuine diversity of opinion, and this is what I thought I was joining – institutions that are diverse not just in terms of race, sex and gender but also in the range of views that exist on campus. I believed, in other words, in the university not so much as an institution but as an idea, in what British statesman Benjamin Disraeli once described as 'places of light, of liberty, and of learning'.

I can even remember imagining at the start of my academic career that my life as a university professor would look something like Russell Crowe's character in *A Beautiful Mind* – the mathematician John Nash, who spent his days advancing the frontiers of know-ledge while wandering around leafy campuses with books under his arm and students hanging on his every word (though, to be fair, Nash later went completely insane). I can also remember thinking that, like those scholars in the past, I'd have complete freedom to write research papers, books and give talks on what-ever topics I wanted, to say whatever was on my mind, without having to worry what others might think. And feeling excited about the fact that I would have respon-sibility for widening rather than narrowing the minds of our young people, the next generation, not least by exposing them to a wide and diverse range of ideas and opinions.

But, over time, as each year replaced the last, as each group of students came and went, as I passed through several universities and made my way through the different stages of an academic career, eventually rising to become one of the youngest professors in the country, I gradually arrived at a very different and a very depressing conclusion. This is not what I had joined at all.

Nearly twenty years to the day since I first graduated from university with an undergraduate degree – and after going on to complete a Master of Arts, a PhD, a postdoctoral fellowship, and then becoming lecturer, senior lecturer and professor – I finally realized that I could no longer avoid what had been staring me in the face: our universities and the wider system of higher education are falling apart. It took me twenty years, in other words, to learn what I am about to tell you. Our universities are no longer interested in their original purpose. They are no longer prioritizing the search for truth, learning, and evidence over dogma. They are no longer protecting and promoting things like free speech and academic freedom. They are no longer opening and challenging the minds of their students. And they are no longer Ivory Towers. Instead, they have morphed into institutions that are delivering, fundamentally, a bad education.

Nor was my view of university life the only thing that shifted over those twenty years. More generally, as I made my way through my academic career, observing what was unfolding on campus, I also found my views about many other issues in society beginning to change – and in profound ways. This is relevant, as we shall see, because it opened my eyes to the true extent to which we are failing to prepare our students and young people for the real world, and why that matters.

When I first began my career as an academic I was, like the vast majority of people in the university class, a fully signed-up member of the liberal left. I used to read and write for the *Guardian*. I voted for the Labour

Party. I worked at left-wing think-tanks. I advised left-wing politicians. I walked around campus wearing T-shirts with Che Guevara on them. I routinely changed my Facebook profile picture to signal my concern about whatever had just upset liberals, and shared their moral outrage over various injustices around the world. I made sure that my tweets included the latest fashionable hashtag. I viewed everything to the right of the centre-left as basically equivalent to 'fascism' and the 'far right'. I routinely complained about conservatives and right-wingers, viewing them as inherently racist and problematic. I spent virtually all my time socializing with other left-leaning academics, which reinforced these views. And, especially when I was on campus, surrounded by other members of the university class, I thought all this was completely and utterly normal.

But today I find myself in a totally different place. Aside from quitting my job and professorship in the universities, many other things in my life have also changed. Today, most of my friends are on the right, not the left. Most of the writers I find interesting are on the right, not the left. Most of the ideas and arguments that I find compelling are on the right, not the left. And now, as much as possible, I go out of my way to avoid socializing with other academics and stepping anywhere near a university campus. Why?

Because all these things are connected; because what

I have watched unfold on campus over the last twenty years also profoundly influenced my views about the direction of the so-called 'liberal' left in Western politics, a movement that much like our universities has increasingly become disconnected from its roots and no longer looks recognizable.

'What happened to you, Matt?' my friends, family and former colleagues are still asking me after my decision to walk away from my professorship. 'When and why did you change your views? Why did you abandon the left? *What happened?*'

Well, as American writer Andrew Sullivan once remarked when he was asked the same question by his old friends on the left,[4] you're asking the wrong question. The question that really needs to be asked if you want to make sense of why I quit my job and completely changed my outlook on life is not 'What happened to me?' No. The question we should be asking the people managing universities, and those who are running the academic departments, teaching students and shaping the minds of our young people, is this: *What the hell happened to you?*

Again, if your natural inclination is to disagree with me on a political level then I urge you to keep reading. Not so that I can change your mind, necessarily, although that would be nice. But so we can at least try and have a serious discussion about the state of our universities and how we might better nurture the bright young minds of today and tomorrow.

There was no single moment when the penny dropped, when I suddenly decided to quit my job. Instead, there was a steady accumulation of shocking moments, events and revelations that simply made it impossible for me to ignore the uncomfortable fact that universities are no longer fit for purpose.

And clearly I'm not the only person who's realized that something is going terribly wrong on campus. In recent years, as I lost faith in higher education, public confidence and trust in these once great and highly respected institutions also collapsed to record lows.

In America, in 2024, the polling company Gallup found that since 2015 the share of Americans who have a 'great deal of confidence' in universities has fallen off a cliff, tumbling from 57% to just 36%. And this decline, for reasons that we'll explore, is especially sharp among Republicans, with the share saying they have 'little or no confidence at all' in universities rocketing from 11% to 50% today.[5]

Around the same time (2023), the *Wall Street Journal* found that a majority of Americans now think negatively about university degrees, with this scepticism strongest among the very people who have degrees, suggesting the crisis on campus is only going to get worse.[6]

In Britain, too, while members of the elite class who graduated from Oxford, Cambridge or one of the other prestigious 'Russell Group' universities routinely use their powerful positions in politics, culture and media to extol the wonders of university education, many other people in the country are clearly having second thoughts. In 2024, remarkably, the polling company YouGov found that most British people now openly reject the suggestion that universities offer 'value for money'. In fact, more than half of all British people, some 52% of them, now say the 'standard of education and the wages graduates earn are not enough to warrant the cost', while more than one in three (38%) think we are 'sending too many people to university'.[7]

Many people in the university class downplay or ignore these findings because they do not fit their narrative that higher education, because of ongoing student demand, is as strong and valuable as ever. But in the polls and surveys it's clear that many people no longer share this view. Like me, they're questioning universities like never before.

On campus, meanwhile, I'm not the only rogue professor who thinks that something has gone terribly wrong. While they might not commit career suicide like me by saying it out loud, I know for a fact that many of my fellow professors would tell you they share my view that universities and the higher education sector in which they sit are now fundamentally broken, maybe even beyond repair.

This is why, across the West, a growing number of renegade scholars have been giving up on the old legacy universities to establish or join entirely new universities that want to lead a return to the things they feel today's universities have forgotten about, such as the search for truth, logic and reason, and immersing students in good faith debate. The University of Austin in Texas, Ralston College in the state of Georgia, the Centre for Heterodox Social Science at the University of Buckingham, and the Peterson Academy, established by the Canadian psychologist Jordan Peterson, are all examples of new universities or research centres that have been specifically founded on a rejection of the current direction of established universities. Historian Niall Ferguson is one figure who has thrown his weight behind the new University of Austin. He writes:

> To the historian's eyes there is something unpleasantly familiar about the patterns of behavior that have, in a matter of a few years, become normal on many campuses. The chanting of slogans. The brandishing of placards. The letters informing on colleagues and classmates. The denunciations of professors to the authorities. The lack of due process. The cancelations. The rehabilitations following abject confessions. The officiousness of

unaccountable bureaucrats. Any student of the totalitarian regimes of the mid-20th century recognizes all this with astonishment. It turns out that it can happen in a free society, too, if institutions and individuals who claim to be liberal choose to behave in an entirely illiberal fashion.[8]

Many other academics and professors, meanwhile, might not be leaving the universities but they are hunkering down on campus, trying to steer clear of the growing chaos and turmoil, counting down the days until their retirement while feeling deeply disillusioned and despondent about the crisis that's now unfolding around them at dizzying speed.

Students, too, have clearly noticed that something is going very wrong on campus. In 2023 it was revealed that student complaints about university courses in England and Wales hit a record high for the fourth year running.[9] Many students, perhaps like their parents, can clearly sense that universities are moving in the wrong rather than the right direction, and that something needs to urgently change.

While members of the university class tell us that the number of students who are enrolling each year is only going up and up, and that everybody will soon belong to the degree-holding class, if you look a little closer you will find that this is rather misleading.

In America, in 2023, the Pew Research Center

pointed out that college enrolments among young Americans, especially young men, have consistently declined over the last decade, with the total number of eighteen- to twenty-four-year-olds enrolling down by 1.2 million from a peak in 2011.[10]

In Britain, too, in 2024, the number of young people applying to university fell for the second year in a row, while the share of students who have enrolled and think university is 'value for money' is sharply down, from 50% in 2013 to 39% in 2024. Furthermore, one in four students now openly admit they thought about leaving university once they arrived on campus, so disillusioned were they with the experience.[11]

Across the West, in other words, while elites remain firmly committed to higher education, lecturing everybody else about why they too should join the degree-holding university class, in recent years it's become crystal clear that rising numbers of scholars, students and citizens are not. Many of them, like me, are turning off universities, worried about what's unfolding on campus and wondering whether university education really is what its proponents claim it to be.

But what's driving the crisis on campus, exactly? Everybody has their own theory. Many of the people you speak to will instantly point to the immense financial pressures on universities that have grown as a result of Brexit, the failure of tuition fees to keep pace with inflation, the impact of the Covid pandemic, a cost-of-living crisis, and worsening relations with foreign powers such as China which have long been a crucial source of international students and, to be blunt, money.

Because of these pressures, many universities can barely afford to keep the lights on. Today, astonishingly, one in four universities in Britain are operating on a financial loss. These pressures are so intense that universities now face an average shortfall of £2,500 on every undergraduate student they recruit, a figure that is forecast to jump to £5,000 by the late 2020s, making many of these institutions unsustainable.[12]

I experienced this first-hand at my last university, the University of Kent, a non-elite institution that like many others further down the league table has been teetering on the brink of bankruptcy for years, owing millions to the banks and pushing academics to take early retirement or redundancy.

Others argue that this crisis is rooted in the massive expansion of the universities, which really took off in the 1990s and propelled people from working-class families like me into higher education.

Like many others in the 2000s and 2010s, I was the first person in my family to go to university. My first lectures were held round the corner from where my working-class grandfather had toiled seven days a week in a steel factory. In short, were it not for the expansion of higher education during the New Labour years then I would probably never have had the chance to go to university.

But, today, it's not hard to find people who will tell you that this expansion went too far, that we are now simply sending too many of our young people into the universities, and that this is devaluing and undermining higher education and wider society. One such voice is British writer David Goodhart, who argues that while the massive expansion of universities has been coordinated and celebrated by the very university class it was designed to benefit, the effects of this expansion have often been negative.[13]

Consider just a few facts that prospective students and their parents will not hear at University Open Days, when professors like me have to act like academic strippers, showing off our teaching, research and buildings in the hope that students and families, while eating cold sandwiches and drinking awful coffee, agree to give us their money. More than one in three of Britain's graduates are now working in jobs that do not require a degree. And this is especially true outside London. While 38% of graduates in the capital are working in jobs that do not require a degree, this increases to 42% in areas outside London and rockets to nearly 60% in places further afield, like Lincolnshire.[14]

At the same time, the financial advantage that comes with having a degree compared to people who do not – the so-called 'graduate premium' – has been declining, not rising. Between Tony Blair coming to power in 1997 and Boris Johnson taking up the reins in 2019, the graduate pay premium fell by 10% across the country, and as much as 20% in some regions, making it harder to make the financial case.

The blunt reality, as the Intergenerational Foundation points out, is that the financial advantage for university graduates is now much lower than it used to be, is lower than what many people in the elite class would like you to think it is, and will likely get even lower in the years ahead, if not disappear completely.[15]

Meanwhile, the obsession with sending everybody to university has left many businesses, industries and regions struggling to find enough people with the right skills to fill vacancies. This point is not lost on ordinary people, many of whom, as I've already noted, are now questioning when and why Western nations became so obsessed with pushing everybody into the university class. According to the British think-tank Onward, two-thirds of all people now think the decision to send young people to university at the expense of sending them to study for technical qualifications has been 'bad for Britain'.[16] And they have a point.

While few of my fellow professors would ever admit it, the blunt reality is that the massive expansion of universities coincided with declining levels of productivity, low growth, rising debt, persistent inequalities, and intensifying social divisions between the university

class and everybody else, with the more socially liberal
if not radically 'woke' progressive outlook of graduates pushing them increasingly apart from the more
conservative-inclined non-graduates who still represent the majority.[17] Is it any coincidence that the likes
of Donald Trump, Nigel Farage, Marine Le Pen and
other populists around the globe attract the bulk of
their support from people who have not gone to university, who do not share the socially liberal values of
the university class, and who often feel that the people
who belong to this class have become increasingly insular, remote, self-serving and adrift from other people?

Still others, such as Harvard philosopher Michael
Sandel in his book *The Tyranny of Merit*, argue that
the shift to a 'university-based meritocracy', where
the only measure of whether someone is considered
'successful' is whether they happen to have gone to the
'right' elite university and have the 'right' degree, is
now creating a much bigger and more visible problem
in the West.[18] Over time, he argues, this has left the
millions of people who chose not to go to university,
or who went to the 'wrong' university and studied the
'wrong' degree, with palpable feelings of humiliation,
shame and resentment, believing they have somehow
'failed' at life. Across the West, this is fuelling what
Sandel calls 'meritocratic hubris', whereby members
of the elite graduate class, who themselves have often
benefited from unfair advantages in life such as being

lucky enough to be born into a rich and connected family, still look down on everybody else with a sense of entitlement and disdain. Given this, he asks, is it really any wonder that so many people are now rebelling against elite members of the university class and their more socially liberal outlook by turning to populist movements?

There's certainly a lot of truth in these arguments, as I hope to show. But while they're important, my more than two decades of working and teaching in the universities lead me to think they are downplaying if not ignoring a much bigger and more profound crisis that is erupting on campus. And this crisis is neither financial nor moral; it is neither about money nor how we organize universities.

It is, instead, deeply political.

My argument is that over the last sixty years our universities and the wider system of higher education have been engulfed by a political revolution which is transforming them for the worse, pushing them away from their original purpose and subjecting an entire generation of students to a bad education, setting them up to fail.

Our universities, in short, have been captured by what I will call in this book a 'new dominant ideology' on campus, a new belief system, a new worldview which is being imposed in top-down fashion on university staff, students and administrators, and which has now fully permeated the culture of academic life.

It's a belief system that has little if any serious interest in the things universities are meant to defend and which they used to promote – free speech and academic freedom, objective scientific evidence, reason, logic, tolerance, debating in good faith, and the exposure of students to a diverse range of ideas and opinions (what John Stuart Mill argued is essential to free speech).

Everybody has a different term for it. Whether we call it 'woke', 'cultural socialism', 'social justice', 'identity politics' or 'progressive illiberalism', the key point is that this belief system is now radically upending and overturning all the things that were once considered central to university life and higher education.

Increasingly, as I've seen first-hand, this ideology is transforming universities – especially the elite ones – into openly political, biased and activist institutions that no longer even try to pretend to be neutral, independent and politically balanced.

Much like universities when they first emerged centuries ago – when they were religious entities – this ideology and its cult-like followers are pushing these institutions to downplay facts, reason, logic, free speech and the need to prioritize scientific knowledge. Instead, they are reshaping our universities around a new religious-style dogma.

And over the last twenty years, as an academic and

then professor, I've been on the front line of this political revolution, watching it mutate and transform from
a noisy but fringe phenomenon on the margins of university life into a dominant force on campus. I've seen it
impose its dogmatic and divisive ideas and theories on
virtually every facet of academia, from student reading
lists to guidance for professors, from staff training to
how universities hire academics.

Not everybody on campus has supported the rise
and creeping spread of this ideology, as we'll see. But,
as I'll show you, because of how our university scholars
have swung sharply to the left, and because of how the
surrounding 'system' of higher education has become
openly political, a minority of activist scholars have
been able to impose this radical belief system on everybody else, staring down more moderate academics,
silencing dissenters and betraying our students.

Inevitably, some people reading this book, especially
if they're on the left, will roll their eyes at this assertion.
Words like 'woke' have become deeply problematic
because they are used by people on the right to discredit
people on the left. And there is truth to this. I try to
avoid using the word 'woke' because I no longer think
it's useful in helping us think clearly about the challenges at hand.

Many people who proudly consider themselves to be
'woke' or focused on achieving 'social justice' are good
people who want to make the world a better place,

eradicate inequality and tackle injustice. These are all noble aims. This book is not an attack on those people. But what is also true is that many of these people might not have set foot on campus for a very long time and so are unfamiliar with the radical changes that have been sweeping through and completely transforming universities since the 1980s and 1990s.

Even more importantly, because of their intense and sincere desire to help minorities, banish racism and make the world a kinder, more tolerant place, they might also have overlooked another crucial point that runs throughout this book: the ideology that's taken over universities and the system of higher education is actually not liberal at all, it is profoundly illiberal. This argument might seem controversial, but among a growing number of scholars and writers who come from across the political spectrum – the right, left and centre – it's not controversial at all. In recent years books and articles by the likes of Francis Fukuyama, Yascha Mounk, Jonathan Haidt, Niall Ferguson, John McWhorter, Eric Kaufmann, Kathleen Stock, Helen Pluckrose, James Lindsay, Nigel Biggar, Greg Lukianoff, Andrew Doyle and Christopher Rufo have contributed to an emerging consensus that what's taken hold of the campus is not just different from classical liberalism but fundamentally opposed to it.[19]

While these people might not always agree on where this ideology came from, whether it's rooted in

Marxism or a radicalization of liberalism, what they all
share is a belief that it now demands our serious attention, not least because of the sheer speed and scale at
which it's upending universities and Western societies
more widely.

And based on my own experience, I agree with them.
One major reason why I decided to quit my job and
write this book is that I wanted to make as many people
as possible aware of how this ideology is wrapping its
tentacles around campuses, suffocating free debate,
imposing a stifling groupthink, silencing its opponents
and corrupting research. In short, it is undermining
and weakening, not strengthening, liberal societies.

Why do I think this? Well, as I used to say to my students, if we want to answer the question we first need
to define the key terms. And a good starting point in
defining this ideology is Professor Eric Kaufmann, a
leading expert. He defines it as being completely organized around 'the sacralisation of racial, sexual, and
gender minorities'.[20] In other words, it's a belief system
that's completely focused on, if not obsessed with, its
core, guiding claim that all racial, sexual and gender
minorities must be considered sacred and untouchable
and must be protected from 'emotional harm', while
the majority must be treated with suspicion, if not con-
tempt, even by themselves.

It's this 'minorities good, majorities bad' reflex,
which lies at the heart of this belief system, that pushes

its followers to be highly sensitive about identity issues. It pushes them, over and over again, to prioritize actual or perceived injustices suffered by minorities at the expense of everyone and everything else, including things that have long underpinned universities and liberal societies such as free speech, bargaining, compromise and tolerance.

Yascha Mounk, a prominent scholar on the centre-left who has advised the likes of Barack Obama and Tony Blair, similarly points out how this ideology is, at its core, 'centrally concerned with the role that identity categories like race, gender, and sexual orientation play in the world'.[21] He traces its rise to the changing priorities of self-described 'liberals' and 'progressives' who today act and think in completely different ways from liberals and left-wingers in the past.

Whereas liberals in the past stressed the importance of broad, universal themes such as individual rights, a common humanity, a shared community, identity and history, tolerance, and people being treated equally before the law, many of today's so-called 'liberals' now embrace a much darker and more dystopian view of our societies and the future. Influenced by the new ideology, they instead see Western societies as being defined by ongoing, never-ending, zero-sum battles for power between minority and majority identity groups, where this power must be redistributed from allegedly 'privileged' majorities to vulnerable minorities, and where the state and institutions, including the universities, must enforce equal outcomes between identity groups.

Why is this problematic? Well, for one thing, as we'll see, while the followers of this ideology claim to be the most liberal and enlightened of all, they feel so intensely about the need to protect minorities that they become deeply intolerant of people who hold different views – especially on university campuses where a diverse range of views are supposed to flourish. Routinely, they seek to disrupt the established order of things, while dismissing and denouncing anybody who challenges them.

On campus, as I've seen first-hand, this intolerance has found its expression in the rampant spread of 'trigger warnings', 'microaggressions', 'safe spaces', preferred gender pronouns, a particularly sharp rise since the 2010s in the number of professors being sanctioned, shut down and silenced simply because of their views, and a similar explosion in the number of university students and professors across the West who now say they are 'self-censoring' – hiding their real views on campus because they fear what might happen if they say them out loud. As Niall Ferguson has pointed out while based in the United States, 'All these terms are routinely deployed on campuses throughout the English-speaking world as part of a sustained campaign to impose ideological conformity in the name of diversity. As a result, it often feels as if there is less free speech and free thought in the American university today than in almost any other institution in the U.S.'[22]

But this glaring intolerance is not the only reason this ideology is deeply problematic. Unlike liberals in the past, who prioritized people's individual rights and believed people should be treated equally, the ideology I have watched take hold of campuses instead pushes staff and students to prioritize people's fixed group identity over who they are as individuals. What matters in this worldview is not who you are – your individual character, values, beliefs – but merely what racial, sexual or gender identity group you happen to belong to. This too represents a radical break from the past. As renowned scholar Francis Fukuyama points out in his book *Liberalism and Its Discontents*, any movement that prioritizes people's fixed group identities over their individual rights has no place within liberalism.[23]

Whereas liberals and civil rights campaigners used to argue that people should not merely be defined by the colour of their skin, their religious beliefs, upbringing or sexual orientation, the ideology that's hijacking campuses rewinds the clock by doing exactly this, telling students that the only interesting and significant thing about them is not their individual achievements and character but merely their race, sex, gender or some other fixed identity, including ones they can't change.

In its most extreme form, as we saw after the attacks against Israel on 7 October 2023, this ideology reduces people to identifying with one of only two groups: either they belong to the white, Western, morally inferior majority, including Jews, which is allegedly 'oppressing' others, or they belong to one of the morally superior minority groups, which according to this ideology must always be considered sacred and protected from any emotional harm because they are allegedly being 'oppressed' by the majority.

Indeed, for many people in the West it was the heinous and horrific attacks against Israel by the Islamist terrorist group Hamas that made the spread of the dominant ideology on campus unavoidable. In the days and weeks that followed, from America to Europe, many people who do not spend their days on campus were visibly shocked and appalled to discover the ideas that have been dominating campuses, and what has been visible to professors like me for years. The outpouring of antisemitism. Professors and their students supporting, if not celebrating, the terrorist attacks by Hamas – or what more than a few of them described as 'resistance'. The death threats, assaults on and intimidation of Jewish students, often by other students. The student groups at the most elite universities in the world, like Harvard, that held Israel 'entirely responsible' for the murder and rape of Jews, committed by Hamas. The leaders of three

Ivy League colleges who were summoned to give evidence to Congress and then refused to unequivocally condemn the antisemitism that was erupting on campuses across America. The astonishing finding in other Western states, like Britain, that 40% of students think the terrorist atrocities by Hamas were 'an understandable act of resistance'.[24] And then watching as the biggest university donors in the world, like hedge fund manager Bill Ackman, started to withdraw their financial support because they no longer had faith in the universities.

Speaking for many ordinary people who, like me, now felt deeply confused and concerned about what was unfolding on campus, American commentator Fareed Zakaria stared into his television camera and asked a question that was very clearly now on the minds of millions of people around the globe. 'How did America's elite universities go from being the kinds of assets the world looks at with admiration and envy to becoming objects of ridicule today?'

It's a good question. And the answer takes us back to the new dominant belief system on campus and why it is so deeply problematic. As social psychologist Jonathan Haidt pointed out in the aftermath of those terrorist attacks, instead of the traditional virtues of university life which first attracted people like me into academic life – truthfulness, free enquiry, persuasion, reasoned argument, equal opportunity, judgement by merit, the pursuit of excellence – this ideology is instead pushing universities into a 'new morality', a new brand of political activism, which is undermining their very purpose.[25]

It's on campus, more than anywhere else, where we see how this ideology conflicts with liberalism. Instead of upholding the 'neutral rules' that have long helped us organize not just universities but liberal democracy – free speech, free expression, equality of opportunity for all, and tolerance – the followers of this ideology, as Yascha Mounk notes, ultimately see these things as unhelpful distractions that merely perpetuate the marginalization of minorities. Minority groups must simply be protected and promoted at all costs, no matter what else happens to be undermined or weakened along the way. If the overriding goal is to create equal outcomes among different identity groups, and ensure that minorities feel 'emotionally safe' at all times, then everything else in society – freedom, excellence, diversity of thought, debate, community, identity and reason – can essentially be sacrificed in the name of pursuing these goals. And this is exactly what's happening on many campuses across the West today.

As we'll see, today's left-leaning professors and students are, by far, the most likely of all to say we should prioritize the protection of minority groups from things like 'hate speech' and feeling offended over the defence of things like free speech. They've also become much more likely to downplay if not ignore any scientific evidence and research which challenges the core claims of this belief system, such as its guiding beliefs that all Western nations are 'institutionally racist', and that minorities are continually being oppressed and discriminated against by majorities in these nations.

Unlike genuine liberals, who appreciate a diverse range of views and opinions, or 'viewpoint diversity', I've instead watched the followers of this ideology routinely stigmatize, silence or simply sack anybody who dares to question or challenge their guiding beliefs. Contrary to what universities are supposed to value and cherish, in other words, this ideology has little if any serious interest in things like objective knowledge, empirical evidence, rigorous debate and reason, especially when they're seen to conflict with its dogma. As we'll see, this is corrupting research, cultivating a stifling groupthink on campus, which is damaging for scholars, students and society, and undermining the very mission of the university – to pursue truth.

It also has little if any interest in maintaining a society where public institutions remain politically neutral and people are treated equally. Instead, because of its obsession with prioritizing minority groups over the majority, this ideology and its followers often argue that past discrimination justifies present discrimination against whites, and that the power of institutions like universities should be used to enforce equal outcomes between different racial, sexual and gender groups. Or as Ibram X. Kendi, a leading light of this ideology, once put it: 'The only remedy to racist discrimination is antiracist discrimination.' In other words, the overriding goal, as Professor Eric Kaufmann points out, is to maximize the position and outcome for what this movement sees as historically marginalized minorities, including women, even if this means discriminating against whites, high-performing students from minority backgrounds, like Asian-American students, and men, such as when deciding who is admitted to university or given prestigious academic jobs.

This also helps to explain its strongly anti-Western and anti-white ethos. Continually attacking, criticizing, questioning and revising national heroes, symbols, history, myths and memories of Western majority groups and essentially recasting them as symbols or tales of racist shame represents an attempt to undercut the pride of the (white) majority group, levelling them down relative to minorities. It's an ideology, in other words, that deliberately cultivates on campus what Eric Kaufmann calls a 'deculturating thrust', encouraging mainly white Western students to repudiate their own history, culture, values and ways of life in the name of protecting and promoting the history, culture, values and ways of life of minorities.[26] Unlike white majorities, minorities are allowed to defend and celebrate their distinctive identities and are prioritized.

Over the last two decades I've watched this divisive, dogmatic and dangerous ideology not only infect every facet of university life but deliver, fundamentally, a bad education to our students.

I've watched its most hardened and committed followers draw on obscure academic theories, such as post-colonial theory, critical race theory (CRT) and radical gender ideology, to crudely declare that all Western nations are 'institutionally racist', to suggest identity politics should be prioritized above objective knowledge, and that our self-identified 'gender identity' must be prioritized over biological reality.

I've watched its followers 'decolonize' reading lists and reframe the West's identity, history, culture and values not as a source of pride and sense of belonging but as a source of shame and embarrassment, which must be repudiated and disowned.

I've watched universities betray their students, families and taxpayers by encouraging the next generation to view highly complex, multi-ethnic societies in crude, simplistic and divisive ways, emboldening them to think the worst of the West and the best of their adversaries, based on a very primitive interpretation of both.

I've watched them push aside all the things universities are supposed to care about, like nuance, complexity and evidence, in favour of their flawed belief that almost every problem in society can be traced back to just one factor: alleged entrenched institutional bias against minority groups.

I've watched them capture and politicize the large and expanding university bureaucracy, reshaping everything from the search for academic jobs and research grants to university places around whatever racial, sexual or gender identity group people belong to, rather than their individual achievements, work and character.

I've watched them dumb down intellectual standards on campus, prioritizing this unscientific political dogma over evidence, rigour, logic and reason, creating a world in which everything from university reading lists to academic hires becomes an openly political project.

Even more worryingly, I've watched them impose this dark and dystopian worldview on our students, the next generation of leaders, exposing them to a belief system that has little interest in those traditional virtues of academic life – truthfulness, free enquiry, persuasion, reasoned argument and debate, equal opportunities for all, assessment by merit, and academic rigour.

And I've watched this movement sacrifice free

speech and academic freedom on the altar of what its
followers call 'social justice', or 'diversity, equality and
inclusion' (DEI) – that when it's a choice between protecting minority groups and upholding free speech,
when it's a choice between protecting the 'emotional
safety' of students and minorities and letting them hear
from a challenging speaker or scholar, our universities
increasingly embrace the former. Dogma now routinely trumps free discussion.

Now, at this point you might think I'm banging a
very personal political drum and simply opposing a set
of ideals that have started to dominate academia, and
wider public life, at the expense of my own. Some readers might think that diversifying university reading
lists, championing minorities and tackling inequalities
in our education system are surely all positive improve-
ments. On the face of it, if handled responsibly, you
might be right; but as it has happened, these developments have come at an enormous and catastrophic cost.

Instead of expanding the minds of students by
exposing them to diverse perspectives, under enormous pressure from this ideology and its followers I've
watched universities silence if not shut down people
who simply express different views, squashing free
speech in the name of protecting minorities and students from 'emotional harm'.

Instead of encouraging people to speak freely and

openly, I've watched them impose a chillingly authoritarian culture of censorship and harassment that would have made the Soviet Union proud. I've watched this movement force thousands of students and scholars to 'self-censor' their views on campus, hiding what they really think because they are too scared to speak their minds in the very institutions that are supposed to allow people to do exactly that.

Instead of protecting and promoting a helpful and constructive vision of 'colour-blind anti-racism', which united an earlier generation of civil rights campaigners like Martin Luther King, I've watched this movement impose a radical and openly racist brand of 'anti-racism', which teaches students that the only way they can become an effective anti-racist is, essentially, by discriminating against white people.

And instead of empowering our students, instead of giving them a sense of agency over their lives, I've watched this ideology incubate them in a dangerous 'culture of victimhood' which incentivizes young people not to see themselves as masters of their own destiny, as individuals with the world at their feet, but as members of some or other victimized identity group.

Now, as a result, having captured and reshaped the institutions, this radical minority of activist scholars and a growing army of university bureaucrats are pushing us further and further into what Yascha Mounk calls 'the identity trap'. It's a trap because while on the surface this ideology appeals strongly to well-meaning liberals who want to tackle injustice and create a society of equals, the outcome will instead be a society that is continuously pushing us apart, encouraging us to view our country in zero-sum terms and reminding us about our differences rather than what we have in common.

I'm certainly not the first person to highlight this problem. In recent years, as I've mentioned, a growing number of writers on both the left and right have written books and given talks about the dangers of this ideology, warning about its creeping influence and impact.

Left-wing and liberal columnists who have not stepped on to a campus for decades and who like to argue that only 'right-wing culture warriors' think this belief system is problematic, including those who will no doubt review this book, are not reading this research.

But while I'm not the first person to point out this problem, I am one of the first to provide an inside view, to tell you what this political and cultural revolution has *really* been like from behind university walls. I've witnessed its evolution while teaching students, undertaking research and helping manage universities, and I've watched many of my friends and colleagues lose their jobs because they dared to challenge the creed, or simply asked questions about it. Some readers will recall the most prominent examples – the likes of Kathleen Stock at Sussex, Nigel Biggar at Oxford, Joanna

Phoenix at the Open University and Noah Carl at Cambridge, people who have been sacked or mistreated on campus because of their unorthodox views. But, as we will see, these cases are just the tip of a much bigger and deeper iceberg.

I'm going to show you exactly how and why this is damaging our universities. Along the way I'll tell you how and why I came to change my own views, too. Because I wasn't always this guy who felt the need to speak out and challenge the prevailing orthodoxy. I used to be happy, content, at peace. Until, that is, I opened my eyes and realized that the problem was not what happened to me but what is now happening to our universities.

The problem, at root, is how this revolution is now rapidly politicizing higher education, harming our students, lowering standards, suffocating free speech, and transforming bastions of learning that used to be the envy of the world into biased institutions that are delivering a bad education.

And I think it's high time that somebody pulled back the curtain so that everybody can see just how bad things have become.

2

Scholars

I can't remember the exact moment when I made the decision to quit my job as a professor, but I can remember the events leading up to it.

The most important, by far, was the seismic Brexit referendum, in 2016, when more than half of all voters in the UK stunned the liberal establishment and expert class by voting to leave the European Union.

I never campaigned for Brexit. But when a majority of my fellow citizens did vote to leave the EU I thought it important to respect their view, not least to safeguard representative democracy. But on my university campus, which during the referendum basically morphed into an outpost of the Remain campaign, this put me in an extremely small minority. Overall, some 90% of academics and professors voted to remain in the European Union, largely because they saw the EU as a bulwark for defending minorities and immigration and because, clearly, many of them saw Brexit as a 'far right' project that posed a major threat to liberal democracy.[1] Their loathing of Brexit was best reflected in my colleague teaching students while wearing a T-shirt which read 'Bollocks to Brexit'. This was considered perfectly acceptable.

Aside from deviating from the cult-like worship of the EU on campus, I also made the mistake of sharing my views publicly, on social media and while writing for national newspapers. I can actually remember thinking, naively, that it was important for professors like me to demonstrate to their students and the wider world that there does exist a diverse and wide range of views on campus.

I was simply not prepared for what happened next. In the weeks, months and years that followed I experienced what I can now only describe as a sustained campaign of abuse, intimidation and harassment, equivalent to how a religious cult treats a heretic. I was accused of being an 'apologist' for the 'far right'. I was denounced as a Tory stooge. I was called an extremist. Even my own head of school liked a tweet insulting me. And in many ways that was the least of it. I experienced coordinated social media 'pile-ons', ironically led by academics who proclaim themselves to be among the most 'liberal' of all. Yet, online, they actively sought to destroy the reputation of anybody who dared to oppose or merely question the new dominant ideology on campus, which Brexit, through its calls for lower immigration and to prioritize the views of the majority, certainly did.

How does this campaign of harassment work, exactly? What happens is that one or two 'gatekeepers' let it be known to more junior academics that somebody has fallen out of favour, that somebody has violated the orthodoxy. The green light is then given for academics to pile in, usually on social media, and a coordinated campaign to try and assassinate somebody's character and reputation begins. For junior academics, there are real incentives for joining in: if you can impress senior scholars by demonstrating your loyalty to the cause and harassing any dissenters then you immediately improve your career prospects.

But this was also deeply hypocritical. Bizarrely, the hostility and harassment came strongest from academics who spent much of their time signalling their allegiance to the latest fashionable cause on campus, such as by showcasing rainbow flags, gender pronouns and the 'correct' hashtags on social media, from #BLM (Black Lives Matter) to #FBPE (Follow Back, Pro-European!), a hashtag that became very popular among members of the university class who were visibly traumatized by the vote for Brexit. Meanwhile, more moderate scholars, cowed by the radical minority of activist scholars, remained completely silent, usually because they too were now fearful of what might happen if they violated the groupthink or irritated the mob.

Looking back now, I realize that the only experience

in my life that came close to the sheer intensity of the hostility and harassment I experienced was during my adolescence, when I was relentlessly bullied at school for being overweight – though even the school bullies were not trying to get me thrown out of school and destroy my entire livelihood.

All this, as you might imagine, had a profoundly negative impact on my health and wellbeing. I didn't sleep properly for months. I drank heavily. I started to see a therapist. I talked at length with a few other renegade professors who had experienced the same thing, one of whom told me he took Valium to sleep at night. And I started to avoid going to campus, whenever possible. Aside from essential teaching and meetings, I turned inwards and away from university life because that life – the life I had once loved – had now become deeply unpleasant and toxic. And simply because I had expressed a view that was held by some 52% of voters.

I began to view my academic career in terms of BB and AB eras – Before Brexit and After Brexit. Before Brexit, I had little trouble doing all the things that are essential for a successful academic career – having my research papers published, securing research grants, being invited into academic networks, giving talks at other universities, and being invited to join prestigious research councils, which decide which academics get what lucrative grants. But After Brexit all these things became much more difficult. One time, when I was asked to give a talk about my research to a company, a disgruntled academic approached the company, generally questioning my invitation to speak. Everything, in other words, became much harder than it ought to have been simply because I had challenged the groupthink.

As the years rolled on, I also became intimately familiar with what are called 'chilling effects', whereby everybody at work just slowly starts to drift away from you and makes it clear you have been ostracized. I was no longer invited to workshops or to give lectures at other universities. I had published two national bestselling books which argued that the people voting for things like Brexit had legitimate grievances over issues such as mass immigration. But, strangely, I was never invited to give talks on them at a single university.

I found it harder to publish academic papers and secure funding for my research, which Before Brexit I'd had no such trouble with. It became more difficult to talk with colleagues, who had once appeared friendly but now seemed wary. I was quietly removed from senior administrative roles in my department, often with no explanation and despite the fact I was a professor in the school and my research papers were among the most highly cited. In turn, this meant I had little influence over things like how we organize our teaching and who we appoint to academic jobs. I was left, in short, with an overwhelming and unavoidable sense that I was now a pariah on campus.

I'm not telling you all this because I want to be seen as a victim. Because I don't. I'm telling you all this because I want you to understand how the university class works and what happens on campus when you are seen to have violated the established orthodoxy. Academics make or break one another under the radar, away from the limelight. If they make it harder for somebody to publish their research papers, present their research, secure funding and access research networks – much of which is done informally, behind the scenes – then, put simply, that person will find it difficult, if not impossible, to climb up the academic ladder.

It might be tempting to read all this and think this is just one story from one disgruntled academic. But this could not be further from the truth. All this was just a symptom of a much deeper and sinister illness that's infecting our universities. As I discovered, while many people in universities like to think they are the most 'liberal' of all, the reality is that the new ideology and its followers routinely harass, intimidate and even fire those who question the religious-style dogma on campus.

What's my evidence for this assertion? Well, for a start, one group that monitors what's happening on campus, Academics for Academic Freedom, have found that in recent years more than 200 academics and speakers have been sacked from their jobs, harassed or disinvited from Britain's universities, almost all of whom violated the new ideology by voicing conservative, gender-critical or other unorthodox views.[2]

In America, too, the Foundation for Individual Rights and Expression (FIRE) has found that while universities have for decades attracted controversy for disinviting or 'no-platforming' controversial speakers, in recent years, as the new ideology went mainstream, the numbers exploded. In fact, they doubled during the 2000s before then surging again in the mid-2010s when cancel culture really took off.[3]

In Britain, one of the most prominent examples is Professor Kathleen Stock, a gender-critical philosopher who was hounded out of her job at Sussex University by pro-trans activists. The campaign, led by students who described themselves as queer, trans and non-binary, started when they criticized the philosopher for signing the declaration of the Women's Human Rights Campaign, which seeks to maintain language protecting women and girls on the basis of sex rather than their self-identified 'gender identity'.

'I went to work as normal,' recalls Stock, 'and saw stickers all over my building about the "transphobic shit that comes out of Kathleen Stock's mouth". That was obviously distressing but the next day it escalated.' Stock arrived on campus to find posters demanding she be sacked: 'Fire Kathleen Stock', 'Kathleen Stock's a Transphobe', 'We're Not Paying Our Fees for Transphobia with Kathleen Stock'.

One day, pro-trans activists, wearing balaclavas, set off flares on campus. 'The imagery was obviously intimidating,' she recalled, 'holding a massive banner saying "Stock Out" while setting off pink and blue flares because those are the colours on the transgender flag . . . I ran back to the station, got the train home, tried to teach a class on Zoom, burst into tears, and my dear students said I must be having a tough day and they let me off. It was the beginning of the end of the campaign to intimidate me out of my job.'[4]

Shockingly, such was the intensity of the campaign against her that Stock was even advised by police to take precautions for her own safety, including installing CCTV at her home and having bodyguards escort her around campus and, astonishingly, while addressing the Oxford Union, a historic bastion of free speech.

And nor was Stock the only one. While it might be tempting to think these are just a few isolated cases, the reality of what's unfolding from one campus to the next is very different. Across the West, many conservative, gender-critical and other scholars who dare to challenge the new ideology – who question the obsession with protecting minority groups from 'emotional harm', who challenge the notion that Western societies are 'institutionally racist', who ask whether people's self-identified 'gender identity' should supersede biological sex, who want to prioritize free speech and free expression over this dogma, or who voice support for conservative causes that are supported by a majority of their fellow citizens, like Brexit – have been bullied, intimidated, harassed or simply thrown off campus. And this, in turn, is leading many students, their parents and concerned citizens to ask themselves the same question: *What the hell is going on?*

The answer is that over the last sixty years universities in the West have been completely, perhaps irrevocably, transformed. They have moved sharply and radically to the left and, as a result, are increasingly betraying their purpose, losing sight of balanced argument and the academic inquisitiveness that values and explores all viewpoints.

This sharp shift to the left, furthermore, is undermining the quality of research and scholarship, eroding free speech by imposing a stifling orthodoxy on campus, and letting down, if not betraying, students.

The university class talks a great deal about the wonders of 'diversity', which has become a 'sacred value' in the new religion on campus, something that can never be questioned and must continuously be celebrated. But as conservative scholar Thomas Sowell once stated, in university the word 'diversity' really only means black leftists, white leftists, female leftists and Hispanic leftists. 'When you hear university academics talk about diversity,' he once quipped, 'ask them how many conservatives are in their sociology department.'

Behind the joke lies a serious point. Routinely, when the university class talks about 'diversity' they are only talking about diversity in terms of race, sex and gender. They never talk about political or ideological diversity, about ensuring there is a genuinely diverse range of theories, values and opinions on campus, and exposing students to these different perspectives.

Clearly, there was never a time when universities were evenly balanced between conservatives and liberals. Writing in 1941, George Orwell famously remarked: 'It is a strange fact, but it is unquestionably true, that almost any English intellectual would feel more ashamed of standing to attention during "God Save the King" than of stealing from a poor box.' It was an early shot at what today we'd call 'the woke elite class'.

But even then the universities were more politically mixed than they are today. In fact, writing even earlier, in 1927, in his book *The Treason of the Intellectuals*, French writer Julien Benda complained that the real problem on campus was not that intellectuals leaned too strongly to the left but that they leaned too strongly to the right. Europe's intellectuals, he warned, were betraying the pursuit of justice and truth by failing to check the passion of the increasingly nationalist masses.[5]

Whereas once upon a time the university class remained utterly dedicated to abstract principles and grand theories, and steered clear of trying to reshape the public in their image, from the end of the nineteenth century, warned Benda, things were starting to change.

From France to Germany, intellectuals were increasingly embracing the political passions they had once rejected. 'These include the drive to action,' wrote Benda, 'the thirst for immediate results, a sole concern for some end goal, disdain for argument, together with excess, hatred, and dogmatic ideas.' And many of the scholars, artists and poets Benda worried about were not aligning themselves with the left but the right, including some of the earliest fascist groups in Europe. From philosophy to art, scholars were working overtime to provide an intellectual justification for the antisemitism, ethnic nationalism and expansionary foreign policy that would later find its expression in the Nazis.

But fast forward to today and things in the universities look very different from both Benda's and Orwell's time. Why? Because whereas the intellectuals who betrayed the universities and their students in the interwar years had often done so from the right, the intellectuals who are betraying the universities today are doing so from the left.

The university class will be livid with me for pointing this out but, as I mentioned in the last chapter, this simply became unavoidable to everybody after the

attacks on Israel on 7 October 2023. While you might
have expected the most educated people on the planet
to condemn the awful atrocities, the murder and rape
of Jews, on one campus after another there was instead
an outpouring of antisemitism and attempts to justify
the actions of Islamist terrorists. As Niall Ferguson
points out, whereas a century ago the likes of Julien
Benda had been deeply alarmed by the extent to which
some scholars were falling over themselves to provide
an intellectual justification for Nazism, since 7 October too many scholars have instead been falling over
themselves to provide a justification for antisemitism
and militant Islamic fundamentalism.[6]

Like what happened when (as I mentioned in the
previous chapter) the leaders of three of the most
elite Ivy League colleges in America – Harvard, Penn
State and Massachusetts Institute of Technology – were
summoned to give testimony to Congress about the pro-
Gaza protests erupting on their campuses. Shockingly,
all three leaders appeared unable to provide a clear
and unambiguous condemnation of the antisemitism
that was on full display at their universities, resulting
in uproar, donors withdrawing their financial support,
and several of the university leaders later resigning in
disgrace.

Or like the academics and postgraduate students at
Exeter University's Institute of Arab and Islamic Studies in Britain, who praised Hamas, cast doubt on the

reported rape of Israeli women, and celebrated the atrocities.[7] Or like the history professor at the elite Cornell University who apologized after saying at a rally on campus that he found the terrorist attack 'exhilarating' and 'energizing', or the climate scientist and professor at Chicago who took to Instagram to describe Israelis as 'pigs', 'savages' and 'excrement'.[8]

Suddenly, the professors and administrators who have a moral panic and intervene in national debates when any other minority group is perceived to have suffered an injustice, however slight, were eerily silent. While many had earlier rushed to signal their moral outrage over events such as the death of George Floyd, issuing statements to align their universities with Black Lives Matter (BLM) – some chapters of which would later voice support for Hamas – Jews, it seemed, did not count. How can we explain things like this?

It's simply impossible to make sense of these events without making sense of how, over the last sixty years, universities in the West have moved sharply to the political left. This has created a dangerous and damaging groupthink on campus, amid which only the pre-approved ideas and beliefs of the new dominant ideology are allowed to flourish, where free speech and academic freedom are eroded, and a radical minority of activist scholars feel emboldened to punish anybody who dares to question or challenge the prevailing orthodoxy.

The university class downplays if not ignores the sheer scale of this shocking political bias. This is because they are part of it, and benefit from it. The evidence for it is now overwhelming. And somebody needs to talk about it openly and honestly.

In America, over the last sixty years, as Professor Eric Kaufmann recounts in his important book *Taboo*: *How Making Race Sacred Produced a Cultural Revolution*, universities have swung sharply to the left. In fact, overall, the ratio of left-wing scholars to right-wing scholars has ballooned, from just 1.5 to 1 in the 1960s to more than 6 to 1 by the 2010s.[9] This of course means that for every one conservative scholar there are six left-wing scholars.

And in some areas this bias is even more shocking. In the social sciences and humanities, the field in which I work, the ratio surged from 3 to 1 in the 1960s to an astonishing 13 to 1 by the 2010s. Conservative scholars are now massively outnumbered by their left-wing counterparts.

Remarkably, in 2016, the year Donald Trump was elected president while tapping into a sense among many ordinary Americans that public institutions were no longer representing their voice and values, one study found that of the more than 7,000 social sciences professors who were teaching and researching at the most elite universities only 314 were Republican. 'People interested in ideological diversity or concerned about the errors of leftist outlooks – including students, parents, donors, and taxpayers,' wrote the authors of the study, 'might find our results deeply troubling.'[10]

And in other areas it's even worse. Mitchell Langbert, a leading expert, has found that in many areas of university life, left-wing scholars do not only dominate but massively outnumber their conservative counterparts, far more so than in the past.

In the US, in fields like theatre studies there are thirty Democrat scholars for every one Republican. In music there are thirty-three Democrats for every one Republican. In art it's 40 to 1, in sociology it's 44 to 1, and in religion it's 70 to 1. Remarkably, in fields like anthropology, communications, gender studies, Africana studies and peace studies, Langbert could not find a single conservative scholar![11]

Universities are supposed to be exposing students to the full range of views and beliefs that exist in wider society. This is how students are encouraged to develop the critical thinking and cognitive skills that help them avoid emotional reasoning and the like. But how can this happen when, as Langbert and his colleagues have shown, in nearly 40% of America's liberal arts colleges there is not a single Republican scholar? How can it be good for students when nearly 80% of academic departments across America either have zero Republican scholars or so few as to make no real difference?[12]

It's a similar story in Britain, where universities used

to be far more politically diverse than they are today. Back in the 1960s, surveys suggested that fewer than half of all academics supported the left-wing Labour Party, while more than one-third supported the Conservative Party. There was still a visible left-wing bias, which is what George Orwell was pointing to while complaining about intellectuals. But since then, the share of right-leaning academics has plummeted, falling below 30% by the 1970s, and then below 20% by the 1980s. By the time of the Conservative Party victory in 2019 more than eight in ten people in the university class supported parties on the liberal left, whether Labour, the Liberal Democrats, the Greens or the Scottish National Party.[13]

Over the last sixty years, in other words, the ratio of left-wing academics to right-wing academics in Britain's universities has rocketed from 1.5 to 1 in favour of the left to 4 to 1 in favour of the left. And in the social sciences, in elite universities, it's closer to 10 to 1.[14]

How is this conducive to the search for truth, evidence and reason? To exposing students to a wide range of viewpoints? And over the last twenty years, these trends became especially visible in my own field of study, the study of politics and international relations.

Ordinarily, you might expect politics students to be taught by professors who come from a range of political backgrounds. After all, shouldn't students be exposed to perspectives from across the political landscape? But this doesn't happen at all.

In fact, routinely, from one academic conference to another, I became used to scholars talking openly about their support not just for remaining in the EU but for an array of left-wing movements, personalities and parties, including the Labour Party, the Liberal Democrats, the Greens, Jeremy Corbyn, the climate extremists Extinction Rebellion, and more. The Conservative Party, meanwhile, was routinely dismissed as 'extremist', 'fascist', or simply 'far right'.

I also became used to attending workshops and conferences that were openly sponsored by left-wing think-tanks, foundations and parties, which would simply never happen the other way round. The academics who were present would routinely attack conservative scholars for 'political bias' yet they had become so immersed in the groupthink they did not see the hypocrisy. Labour MPs and left-wing politicians from other countries would also sometimes appear at these events as guest non-academic speakers. This was considered entirely normal and acceptable, encouraged even. But when I asked prominent Conservative politician and Brexit campaigner Daniel Hannan to address a conference in the same capacity, academics literally walked out of the room halfway through to signal their disgust. They could not even handle being in the same room as somebody who voiced pro-Brexit views.

I also became used, from one election to the next, to watching my fellow academics use their social media accounts, lectures and office hours to signal their open support for a variety of left-wing parties and radically progressive social movements, from Black Lives Matter to Follow Back, Pro-European! Meanwhile, anything and everything to the right of the Labour Party was considered 'racist', 'deviant' or 'far right'.

Nor did they think it odd when fellow scholars worked part-time for the Labour Party or the Liberal Democrats, or established political consultancy companies with Labour MPs. This was welcomed, encouraged even, such as the politics professors who helped launch the Social Democratic Party (SDP) in the 1980s. Had anybody worked this closely for the Republicans or Conservatives, the moral outrage and panic would have been overwhelming. The double standards became impossible to avoid.

Much of this makes sense when you look at the data on who is teaching and working in the field of politics on campus. One study by Harvard professor Pippa Norris found that no less than 72% of politics lecturers and professors put themselves on the left wing, with 14% openly describing themselves as 'far left'.[15]

A few years ago, I became so concerned about what was taking place on campus that I decided to carry out my own study of academics who were teaching and working at the most elite universities in the world, from Harvard to Oxford. Astonishingly, I found that more than three-quarters of those who responded to my survey, 76%, put themselves on the left, with 21% of them openly identifying as 'far left'. Just one in ten of the academics and professors working in the world's most elite universities put themselves on the right.[16]

And that wasn't all. I also found big differences in the political outlook of these scholars, with those on the left exhibiting more hostility towards those on the right than vice versa: the vast majority of academics who leaned left also held a strongly negative view of right-wing voters, while the few academics who leaned to the right held a generally neutral or even favourable view of left-wing voters.

The most visible hostility and intolerance towards people who hold different views, in other words, was coming from the very people who simultaneously claimed to be the most educated, enlightened and tolerant of all. And this has since been underlined by an important new study.

In his book *Liberal Bullies*, published in 2024, Professor of Psychology Luke Conway marshals a considerable amount of evidence to show how liberals are often just as likely as conservatives to want authority figures to 'crush their enemies and silence their opponents'.[17] In fact, if anything, Conway finds that liberals are *more* prone to authoritarian beliefs than conservatives are, with an alarmingly large number of liberals displaying the dogmatic, rigid, black-and-white thinking they often associate with their populist opponents.

Why does all this matter, you might ask? What's the problem with universities leaning so strongly in only one political direction? Well, it matters for several reasons, all of which are undermining the institutions themselves and the quality of higher education.

For a start, these trends have left the university class utterly disconnected from the societies that surround them. In Britain, while around half of all people support conservative parties, less than 12% of the university class does. And while more than half of all voters in Britain supported Brexit, only 10% of academics did. As political debates in the West have become as much about culture as economics, in other words, the universities have drifted further away from the average voter.

What this reflects is a deeper problem. As they've drifted leftwards, universities have increasingly morphed into what are called 'monocultures' – institutions where only a single set of ideas, beliefs, assumptions and priorities are allowed to flourish. This has empowered a much more radical minority of activist scholars to impose themselves on academic departments, committees and campus life.

Major surveys by think-tanks like More In Common show that in wider society only around 10–15% of people in the West share the views of the 'radical progressives' who dominate campus, people who typically want to increase immigration, say they would prioritize the protection of minorities over defending free speech, believe that someone's self-identified 'gender identity' must supersede their biological sex, and strongly agree that Western states are systemically racist.

But on campus, amid a strong left-wing bias, there is very little opposition to these more radical activists, who feel free to impose their will on others. This is why, so often on campuses today, people who hold different views or challenge this monoculture are finding themselves being pushed to the very margins of university life, encouraged to stay quiet if not completely silent.

The end result of all this is a damaging and stifling groupthink which erodes free speech and the academic freedom of scholars to research and say whatever they like, all of which was once considered absolutely central to university life and higher education.

As Professor Eric Kaufmann tracks in his detailed study, the rise of this culture of censorship and cancellation began in the 1960s, when small numbers of activists began their move on to campus. These revolutionary radicals, who often aligned themselves with groups such as the Black Panthers, were assisted by a much larger group of more moderate liberal scholars who sympathized with minorities, felt a sense of guilt about how they had been treated in the past, and were instinctively hostile towards majority groups and conservatives. This wider 'circle of tacit support' helped the radicals break through.

This radical minority then used demonstrations, disruptions and moral blackmail to intimidate others. In this way, they established a beachhead on campus, from which they launched a much wider attack on higher education. Increasingly, as their numbers grew, they took over key academic and administrative positions in the expanding university bureaucracy, hired their own, pushed departments to become more political, and openly opposed scholars with different views.

Since then, the sharp leftward shift, the strong political bias on campus, has been corrupting research and undermining the credibility of universities that in public claim to prioritize the pursuit of truth but which in reality have become activist institutions, interested only in a very narrow set of ideas that conform to and confirm a specific worldview.

Human beings have always struggled with the pursuit of truth because we are prone to things like 'confirmation bias', where we seek out evidence that confirms our beliefs; 'motivated reasoning', where we interpret things in a way that is consistent with our beliefs; tribalism, where we place ourselves into competing groups; and the worshipping of sacred values, where we simply believe that some values are more important than others. The only way of disrupting

these unhelpful thought patterns is by exposing ourselves, regularly, to alternative viewpoints, to rigorous
debate, and by protecting the free speech that's needed
to do just this.

But these things do not happen when everybody
around you shares the same values, the same attitudes,
the same political loyalties, the same assumptions, the
same research interests. When this happens, when universities become monocultures, it becomes difficult
if not impossible to pursue truth and reason. When
universities are taken over in this way they end up promoting a warped and biased view of the world, which
is then passed on to students before trickling out into
wider society.

In many Western states, for example, lowering the
level of immigration, deporting illegal migrants and
pushing back against various so-called 'woke' policies
are supported by majorities of the population.

In 2024, in Britain, two-thirds of all people told
pollsters YouGov that immigration into the country
had been 'too high', 67% would support increasing
deportations of illegal migrants, and 56% think that
public spaces should have separate toilets for men and
women.[18]

But in the insular, stifling and homogeneous world
on campus, these views are often considered 'deviant', 'racist', 'hateful' or 'transphobic'. Yet while it's
simply assumed people on the right are more biased,

authoritarian and prejudiced than people on the left, the alternative possibility, that people on the left are more biased, authoritarian and prejudiced (which studies like that by Luke Conway suggest), is ignored.

Groupthink is also damaging because it undermines the quality of research. Despite many social problems being the result of a complex interplay of factors, from economic deprivation to family breakdown, in universities it's often assumed that social problems are the result of just one variable – racism and discrimination among whites. To argue against this, to point out that differences in outcomes among different groups might owe more to things such as higher rates of family breakdown among some minority groups, or different cultural values, is considered tantamount to blasphemy.

Between 2010 and 2015, I taught at the University of Nottingham, one of the country's elite 'Russell Group' universities. But a few years ago it hit the news for the wrong reasons after the university decided to rescind its offer of an honorary PhD to the black British campaigner Tony Sewell, who has spent his life working to help left-behind black children. Why? Because Sewell had dared to challenge this guiding belief in the new dominant ideology, that any differences in outcomes among identity groups must be because of racism and discrimination against minorities. Instead, while overseeing a government commission, Sewell painted a much more nuanced picture of life in Britain. He pointed, rightly in my view, to how well some children from minority ethnic backgrounds are now performing at every level of the education system, while also pointing to the influence of factors which have nothing to do with racism and discrimination, for instance the much higher rates of family issues among some minority groups, such as British Afro-Caribbean families, where fathers are often absent.

Amid feverish support at the time for Black Lives Matter, some organizers of which were subsequently found guilty of fraud and connected with support for the violent Islamist terrorists Hamas, Nottingham branded Sewell a 'subject of political controversy' and withdrew its offer of an honorary doctorate. Yet, interestingly, this did not stop Nottingham handing out honorary degrees to senior Chinese communists and corrupt politicians in Malaysia, where it happened to have lucrative overseas campuses – a point we will return to.

This strong left-wing bias is also damaging because it encourages scholars to focus heavily, if not exclusively, on research questions and findings which support the established groupthink, while downplaying, refuting or ignoring findings that might challenge it.

In the field of sociology, for example, where left-liberal values dominate, the term 'white privilege' has gone mainstream to refer to the allegedly unearned advantages whites enjoy because of their skin colour and majority status. But as some renegade scholars note, this implies whites are advantaged relative to all other groups when in fact, for example, Asian Americans are more advantaged than whites by having things like higher average incomes, better outcomes in the education system, and a lower likelihood of experiencing crime.[19]

Groupthink also leads scholars to prematurely 'close' entire areas of research, declaring a debate settled simply because the first findings seem to confirm their existing views. This can lead to research being promoted or dismissed without proper academic rigour. One example of this came in 2014, when a graduate student named Michael LaCour published a paper that claimed to show people's views about gay marriage could be changed by having short conversations with gay canvassers, but not straight canvassers. If the canvasser talked to people for twenty minutes, telling them they were gay, then they could convert opponents of gay marriage into supporters. The findings were music to the ears of the liberal progressive scholars who dominate campuses, and were covered extensively by the *New York Times*, the *Washington Post*, the *Wall Street Journal* and *The Economist*. The paper itself was published in the prestigious journal *Science*, underlining how LaCour was embraced by the academic elite and could look forward to a very promising career.

The only problem was that the study wasn't real. The data had been made up. In fact no data had been collected. And the survey company listed in the study said it had never been hired.

Yet while the study was later retracted and LaCour's academic career was left in ruins, the scandal was significant for bigger reasons. As the *Wall Street Journal* noted at the time, the reason why the study was originally welcomed and celebrated by the academic community is because it 'flattered the ideological sensibilities of liberals, who tend to believe that resistance to gay marriage can only be the artifact of ignorance or prejudice, not moral or religious conviction. Mr LaCour's findings let them claim that science had proved them right.'

Furthermore, the scandal reflected a wider phenomenon in the social sciences, 'which often seem to exist so liberals can claim that "studies show" some political assertion to be empirical. Thus they can recast stubborn political debates about philosophy and values as disputes over facts that can be resolved by science.'[20]

Another example of how groupthink leads scholars to accept questionable if not deeply flawed and low-quality research because it supports their own politics is the Grievance Studies Affair. This saw three scholars – Peter Boghossian, James Lindsay and Helen Pluckrose – throw light on the sheer scale at which universities have been captured by the new ideology and how, in turn, this has been dramatically lowering intellectual standards and research integrity.

Sick of watching academics prioritize quasi-religious dogma over evidence and truth, the hoaxers submitted deliberately fraudulent papers to academic journals with titles such as 'The Conceptual Penis as a Social Construct' (which argued that penises are not 'male' but social constructs) and 'Human Reactions to Rape Culture and Queer Performativity at the Dog Park' (which argued that dog parks are 'rape-condoning spaces' and suggested ways of tackling 'toxic masculinity'). By having these papers published in peer-reviewed academic journals, the hoaxers pulled back the curtain to reveal the extent to which scholars and journal editors will publish absurd low-quality research simply because it appears to corroborate their own beliefs.

Consider, too, what happened to African American scholar Roland Fryer who, while working at Harvard, in 2016 released a study which showed that while African Americans and Hispanics were more likely to experience force during their interactions with police there was not 'any racial bias in police shootings'. When Fryer talked about his findings his colleagues took him to one side and warned him not to publish them. 'You'll ruin your career,' they said.[21] He didn't listen to them and decided to publish the paper because, like all good academics, he prioritized truth over dogma. The paper was published with a 150-page statistical appendix.

But within minutes of sharing it, he received his first criticism: 'This is full of shit. Doesn't make any sense.' Astonishingly, in the weeks that followed Fryer was forced to live under police protection due to the violent threats made against him.

These are all examples of a deeper problem with monocultures. As Jonathan Rauch points out in his book *The Constitution of Knowledge*, when there is such a glaring lack of political diversity on campus, when institutions swing so sharply to the left, scholars who do not conform with the orthodoxy often end up, like me, shunned, silenced, stigmatized, shut down and even sacked for their political views.[22]

This cancel culture on campus, Professor Eric Kaufmann notes, usually takes two forms. First, there is 'institutional punishment', which is what happens when universities simply impose top-down censorship on scholars who challenge the new religion, such as when Sussex made philosopher Kathleen Stock's work life intolerable.

The second is what Kaufmann calls 'political discrimination', which is a more informal and softer form of peer pressure on scholars not to deviate from the established orthodoxy on campus. Instead of firing scholars, this involves damaging their reputations through online mobbings on social media, by shunning them in academic networks, by making it harder for them to publish their research or secure research grants simply because they hold different political views, by marginalizing and ostracizing them on campus, and compelling them to 'self-censor', hiding their real views because they fear what might happen to their social standing and career if they don't.

I saw this first-hand in Britain when, in 2018, another critical moment in my journey towards quitting my professorship took place. That was when a young and promising scholar named Noah Carl was thrown out of Cambridge and had his world turned upside down.

Carl, a moderate conservative, made the mistake of studying a controversial topic that was definitely considered completely off-limits on campus: differences in levels of intelligence among ethnic groups. He had never actually published research papers on race and intelligence, though he had published one ethics paper suggesting there are costs as well as benefits to stifling debate on controversial topics. Only two of his more than thirty published papers dealt with the topic of intelligence, the rest exploring issues such as people's views of immigration, Brexit, and British politics. Nonetheless, when Carl's research interests became known, he was attacked from all sides.

More than 1,400 scholars and students from around the globe, many of whom neither worked in Carl's area of research nor knew him personally, rushed to sign an open letter denouncing the young scholar for conducting 'racist pseudoscience', attending a 'discredited' conference on intelligence, and publishing articles that were later cited by far right groups. Amid campus protests, students and scholars lobbied Noah Carl's employer, St Edmund's College, to demand that his prestigious research fellowship be terminated.

The master of the college, Matthew Bullock, a former banker, caved. Carl was ousted and his academic career destroyed. Bullock, meanwhile, apologized to Cambridge students for the 'hurt and offence' caused, underlining how free speech and the freedom of academics to study whatever they want were sacrificed on the altar of 'social justice' ideology and its obsession with protecting students and minorities from 'emotional harm'.

The story of Noah Carl reflects how academics routinely move to isolate and exclude perceived heretics. It usually begins with a handful of students complaining about their 'emotional safety' on campus. It then progresses to a very public 'open letter', signed by more senior scholars, which is used to humiliate and intimidate the scholar who has challenged groupthink. Public letters discourage others from getting involved, sending nonconformists and moderates a warning they could be next if they step out of line. These letters also shut down the prospect of good faith debate, making it impossible to have a measured discussion and for the person under fire to offer a serious response. The public letters and online mobbings usually include misleading claims, ad hominem attacks and sweeping statements about the person's work and character, many of which are made by scholars who work in different areas of research or Master's and PhD students who are simply not qualified to evaluate the research being discussed.

Then comes the 'guilt by association' charge – that scholars must be fully accountable for whoever engages with their research or happens to sit alongside them at an academic conference: Noah Carl, for example, was mobbed by students and staff simply for attending a research conference that included people with a wide range of views.

And then, eventually, comes the university bureaucrat or college master who caves to these dogmatic demands from the mob, usually citing concerns about 'student satisfaction', the need to protect students from 'emotional harm', and defending the university's reputation.

What's not talked about at this point is the importance of defending 'academic freedom' – the freedom of scholars to research whatever they want in the pursuit of truth – as well as the need to expose students to a range of views, however uncomfortable they might find them.

What your own thoughts are about Noah Carl's research interests is not the point. The point is that it should be entirely legitimate and acceptable to research and debate subjects like race and intelligence within a university setting, where the search for truth must always be prioritized over politically correct opinions. The outcome of such a debate might have challenged Carl's findings, but that should have been achieved through proper objective scientific enquiry and should not have come at any personal cost to Carl himself.

I was appalled by the treatment of Noah Carl and the refusal of the vast majority of my academic colleagues to speak out. Deep down, most of them knew it was profoundly wrong yet still they sat watching a young scholar be bullied and harassed out of the university while saying nothing at all. It was, as I said, another major turning point for me.

So too was what happened in 2018 when a few colleagues and I decided to arrange a discussion in London on the topic of immigration, an issue that much of the research showed had driven a large number of people to vote for Brexit two years earlier.[23] We brought together a diverse panel of speakers from the left and right, wanting to explore why so many people in the country felt under threat from mass immigration.

But amid the new groupthink on campus, even hosting the debate was considered blasphemous. Even before a word had been spoken, hundreds of self-described 'academics and activists' signed an open, public letter suggesting that the debate had been 'framed within the terms of white supremacist discourse'.[24] It was another example of how today's scholars, rather than tolerating debate and exposing people to a wide range of views, instead move to try to silence and stigmatize those they find challenging.

The beliefs that now dominate campuses are not just religious and political in nature. They are also wrapped up with academia's intense and never-ending quest for social status and esteem from other members of the university class. Cambridge graduate Rob Henderson has written eloquently about how today's elite class, especially those who work in the most prestigious universities, increasingly define themselves by what he calls 'luxury beliefs'.[25]

Luxury beliefs are ideas and opinions that are aggressively promoted by the elite class, especially on elite campuses, because they confer social status and esteem on members of that elite class while inflicting heavy costs on people who do not belong to it.

In the aftermath of the death of George Floyd in 2020, countless universities and professors joined the rush to express solidarity with Black Lives Matter, issuing statements as though they were elected governments rather than politically neutral institutions. Affluent professors with tenured jobs at elite universities, most of whom live in similarly affluent and heavily white neighbourhoods, signed open letters calling on governments to 'defund the police', while those who asked questions or voiced opposition were vilified.

One example was Professor Harald Uhlig, at the University of Chicago, who suddenly found himself attacked on all sides after criticizing Black Lives Matter and the movement to Defund the Police, with many prominent professors calling on him to be sacked and urging others to sign, once again, the ever-present online petition. He was placed on leave as editor of a prestigious academic journal, and though he was later reinstated, his name was still dragged through the mud.

Many of the professors who rallied behind calls to defund the police and sack the likes of Uhlig knew they were not the people living in the low-income, crime-ridden and mainly black neighbourhoods that would have to deal with the consequences of reduced police powers or growing mistrust of police authority. While the luxury belief class continued to demand policies that won them more social status and applause from other members of the elite class, especially on social media, studies later found that the widespread police pullback led to a sharp decline in people being arrested for property crime and a sharp increase in murder.

In fact, one study in America estimates that calls to defund the police led to 3,000 additional murders that would not otherwise have happened – not far off the number of people killed during 9/11.[26]

Another example of luxury beliefs that thrive on campus but work less well in the real world is the attack on the traditional constructs of family and monogamy, typically in the name of promoting or protecting other relationship preferences. As Rob Henderson – who, like me, comes from a broken home – noted, when he arrived at the prestigious Yale University he discovered lots of people from stable two-parent families in the elite class insisting that traditional families were 'old-fashioned' and society should 'evolve' beyond them. Yet, at the same time, these people ignored or downplayed a large body of evidence which people from single-parent homes know to be true – namely, that children from these backgrounds consistently perform worse in the education system and are far more prone to a wide range of social and mental problems, including drug and alcohol addiction, criminality and unemployment.

Another luxury belief that thrives on campus, and which Henderson also struggled with because he grew up around lots of very poor white people, is 'white privilege'. Once again, affluent white college graduates are the most passionately supportive of this idea because they are the least likely to incur the costs for promoting it. While they raise their social status among other members of the elite class by reflecting on their 'whiteness' or 'white privilege', when policies are implemented to combat these 'problems' it simply won't be the Oxford,

Harvard or Yale graduates who are harmed, it will be poor whites who are already left behind economically and socially. In fact, recent studies suggest that training people in ideas like white privilege makes them less sympathetic towards working-class whites.[27] As Henderson notes:

> The upper class promotes abolishing the police or decriminalising drugs or white privilege because it advances their social standing. The logic is akin to conspicuous consumption: if you're a student who has a large subsidy from your parents and I do not, you can afford to waste $900 and I can't, so wearing a Canada Goose jacket is a good way of advertising your superior wealth and status. Proposing policies that will cost you as a member of the upper class less than they would cost me serves the same function. Advocating for sexual promiscuity, drug experimentation or abolishing the police are good ways of advertising your membership of the elite because, thanks to your wealth and social connections, they will cost you less than me.

In the same way, demonstrating your awareness of key concepts in the new ideology, such as white privilege, whiteness, cisgender and allyship, displaying gender pronouns in your email signature, demanding that your department 'decolonize' its reading lists and declaring the West to be 'institutionally racist', are also markers that you belong to the new luxury belief class. Much of this is about signalling one's membership of the high-status elite, one's sense of moral righteousness, one's commitment to the new ideology.

And like all good religions, so too is demonstrating your dislike (if not hatred) of perceived non-believers – the heretics, the people who are seen to be promoting a different set of views on campus. From Noah Carl to Roland Fryer, from Kathleen Stock to what I experienced, in recent years it's become crystal clear that the freedoms that were once considered central to higher education – to speak freely, to teach diverse perspectives, to enjoy academic liberty – are under serious threat.

In fact so bad have things become in Britain that in 2023 the Academic Freedom Index (a measure of how much scope a university has to research and teach what it wants) concluded that academic freedom has been significantly eroded over the last ten years, with Britain now ranked sixtieth in the world, well below nearly every country in Europe.[28] One big reason for this is the strong left-wing bias and groupthink on campus which creates a hostile climate for scholars who hold different views.

Other academics will tell you this is not happening, or that my examples are blown out of proportion, used by 'right-wing culture warriors' to sow division. But this is not true. There is an overwhelming amount of evidence that people who violate the dominant ideology on campus are severely punished, removed from the public square, hounded from office or simply scared into silence.

In 2021, in the first study of its kind, the Center for the Study of Partisanship and Ideology uncovered widespread evidence of a hostile environment for scholars who do not follow the orthodoxy. Across America, Canada and Britain, significant numbers of academics openly admitted they would discriminate against conservative scholars when hiring and promoting colleagues, when assessing whether or not to award them prestigious grants, and when deciding whether or not to publish their academic papers, all of which are absolutely central to carving out a successful academic career.[29]

In America, since the 2010s, studies have likewise tracked a sharp rise in the number of academics who have been investigated, penalized and/or sanctioned by students or staff simply because of something they said in class or wrote on social media. And most of these attempted cancellations have been led by scholars on the left.[30]

And much of this appears to be getting worse, not better. Between the years 2000 and 2022, the Foundation for Individual Rights and Expression

(FIRE) found that the number of attempts to sanction and punish scholars for speech that would otherwise be protected by America's First Amendment had rocketed from just four cases to nearly 150, most of which were, once again, driven by scholars and students on the left, not the right.

And this harassment has been most visible at elite universities. In America, a striking number of attempts to sanction scholars who fall foul of the groupthink has been recorded at elite Ivy League colleges Harvard, Stanford, UCLA, Georgetown, Columbia and Pennsylvania – ironically many of the same ones where administrators refused to condemn the outpouring of antisemitism in the wake of the Hamas attacks of October 2023.[31] In 2024, as shocking cases such as the poor treatment of Roland Fryer reflect, Harvard received the lowest possible score of zero, because it was, concluded the study, 'the only school with an "Abysmal" speech climate rating'.[32]

In fact, even Eric Kaufmann, who has done more than most to track these trends, has ironically experienced the very intolerance and harassment he has been warning about through his detailed research.

In 2023, Kaufmann was forced to abandon his secure professorship at Birkbeck, University of London, after life on campus became intolerable. Kaufmann had not only violated the new orthodoxy by pointing to its intolerance but had also shown how people who feel

anxious over immigration were motivated by legitimate concerns. 'This public profile,' he wrote, 'placed
me in the crosshairs of a well-organised network of
radical students and academics inside and outside the
university who took it upon themselves to police the
boundaries of acceptable debate on campus.'

He became the target of continual pile-ons on social
media, organized by activist scholars and students
in the student union. They signed an open letter,
calling on him to be fired. One colleague wrote an
open letter about why she was leaving the university,
claiming Kaufmann's research and views had created
a hostile and 'emotionally challenging' environment.
She now works at a neighbouring university.

By whipping up an online frenzy an activist minority
makes a scholar radioactive before they are even able to
respond, while protests, letters and complaints almost
always turn into formal investigations, which bring
more stress. 'Until you have received an email informing
you that you are under investigation and must attend
a tribunal,' wrote Kaufmann, 'you cannot understand
the psychological impact of this tactic. The spectre of
unspecified penalties sets the mind racing towards the
possibility of termination – this in a collegiate profes-
sion where there are hundreds of applications for each
post and gossip travels fast. Once out, getting back in is
near-impossible. The process is the punishment.'

What Kaufmann experienced is exactly what his

research had suggested is now becoming mainstream on campus: political minorities, including conservatives, routinely face a hostile environment.

And the evidence backs him up. Remarkably, in America and Canada, more than four in ten scholars openly say they would not hire somebody who voted for Trump, while one in three scholars in Britain say they would not hire somebody who voted for Brexit.[33]

Furthermore, fewer than half of British academics say they'd feel comfortable sitting next to somebody who had voted for Brexit at lunch (which might explain the reaction to me on campus), while one in three say the same about people who express gender-critical views, who disagree with the idea that somebody's gender identity should supersede their biological sex. Indeed, it's important to underline that it's not only conservative scholars who suffer from this hostile environment. The political crisis on campus is not just a 'left versus right' issue, with many gender-critical scholars facing the same intense hostility and harassment, regardless of their wider political inclinations.

There are now many examples of 'gender-critical' scholars being harassed, bullied, ostracized or sacked because of their views, much of this also involving online mobbings by people who like to think of themselves as liberal-minded social justice campaigners. In America, for example, just 28% of academics on campus say they would feel comfortable having lunch with a scholar who opposes the idea of transgender women accessing shelters for women.[34]

And there are countless examples of how this intolerance manifests on campus. Jo Phoenix, Professor of Criminology at Open University, was forced to bring an employment tribunal claim after a public campaign of harassment made her life unbearable. Phoenix had made the mistake of expressing concern about the silencing of debate on campus about trans issues, also criticizing the influence of activist campaign group Stonewall in the universities. She also suggested that biological males should not be allowed in female prisons, and set up a gender-critical research network to discuss and debate these issues.

In response, nearly 400 academics signed an open letter calling her research 'transphobic' and launched a targeted campaign against her. A senior university manager told her she was 'like the racist uncle at the Christmas dinner table', and she was told not to speak about her work in departmental meetings. Open University was later found liable on twenty-five counts of belief discrimination and harassment.

Feminist Linda Bellos similarly had her invitation to speak at the Cambridge college Peterhouse withdrawn because of concerns about the emotional safety of students. 'I'm sorry but we've decided not to host you,' wrote Ailish Maroof, co-president of the 'gender and feminism' student society. 'I too believe in freedom of expression, however Peterhouse is as much a home as it is a college. The welfare of our students in this instance has to come first.'

Researcher Heather Brunskell-Evans, at King's College London, who was also a spokeswoman for the Women's Equality Party, was no-platformed by students after she questioned gender ideology on radio. The event was cancelled because of concerns her views 'would violate the student union's "Safe Space" policy'.

James Caspian, a psychologist who wanted to study people who regret having undergone gender reassignment, was told by his university that the subject was 'potentially politically incorrect'.

A senior professor and university administrator at Imperial College London, Simone Buitendijk, was forced to issue a 'grovelling apology' after more than eighty students signed an open letter claiming she had shared articles and liked content that questioned gender ideology. In something reminiscent of a Soviet show trial, Professor Buitendijk publicly promised to stop all engagement with this content online, while ICL issued a statement that read: 'We are pleased that a significant body of students has expressed support for the trans community in response to this issue.'

The list goes on and on. The academic at Glasgow University who was threatened with being sacked as an editor of a prestigious academic journal after sharing her view that the imposition of gender ideology training on campus presented anti-scientific claims as objective fact.

The academic whose research article was branded 'transphobic' by colleagues because it used the word 'women' to refer to people born female, and who required additional security when presenting the paper.

Member of the House of Lords Baroness Claire Fox, who found herself disinvited from a university debating society event at Royal Holloway on (ironically) the importance of discussion, after retweeting a joke by the comedian Ricky Gervais about 'old-fashioned women' having wombs and new women having 'beards and cocks'.

The University of Edinburgh event on how gender issues are taught in Scotland's schools that was branded 'transphobic' by the university's Staff Pride Network and cancelled after organizers were told the safety of its female speakers could not be guaranteed.

These examples of gender-critical scholars being silenced and shut down are problematic not only because of the impact on individual scholars – who in a university setting should have every right to critique and debate subjects such as radical gender ideology, asking to what extent it is rooted in objective scientific knowledge – but because they reflect the much broader assault on academic freedom and free speech that's now taking place in the West, especially when it involves nonconformist scholars who do not follow the dominant ideology.

And the trend is wider than that. Consistently, across the West, Labour voters, Democrat voters, Remainers and self-defined 'liberals' are the most likely to be hostile towards people with different views. As I experienced personally, in the aftermath of Brexit and the election of Donald Trump, in 2016, when, instead of exploring people's concerns, the left-leaning elite chose to label their fellow citizens racists, bigots, deplorables and morons, confirming the suspicion among many that the elite class is neither interested in them nor even likes them.

In fact, like that study by psychologist Luke Conway, research suggests that especially in elite institutions people on the left are more intolerant of people on the right than vice versa, being much more likely to unfriend, block, disassociate and distance themselves from people who voice different political views from their own.[35]

In America, the reliable Pew Research Center finds that while only 26% of Facebook users have hidden, blocked, unfriended or stopped following somebody because they disagreed with their online posts about politics, among self-described 'consistent liberals' the figure rockets to 44%.[36]

In Britain, too, while only 9% of Brexit voters said they would mind if one of their relatives married somebody who had voted to remain in the European Union, nearly 40% of Remain voters, who routinely presented themselves as the most liberal and tolerant of all, said they would mind if one of their relatives married somebody who had voted to leave. Many self-described liberals felt profoundly uneasy about the idea of one of their relatives marrying a Brexit voter, a Trump voter, or somebody who holds gender-critical views.[37]

Typical of this worldview was a Senior Lecturer in Philosophy at Royal Holloway who after the Conservative Party's election victory in 2015 took to social media to express a common view on campus: 'If you're a Conservative, I'm not your friend . . . One of the first things I did after seeing the depressing election news this morning was check to see which of my Facebook friends "like" the pages of the Conservatives or David Cameron, and unfriend them.'[38]

As American journalist Leighton Woodhouse points out, what this reflects is the rise of a new elite class that is deeply intolerant of people who hold different political beliefs from their own, who silence and stigmatize others partly to try and consolidate their grip over the institutions and enforce the groupthink. 'The children of the ruling class,' Woodhouse writes, 'have colonized the left, and are using its moral language to malign the broader . . . public as a bigoted, ignorant, dangerous mob. To protect the "vulnerable" and "marginalized" from this threat, they demand the ideological allegiance of every elite political, cultural, and media institution; the social and professional ostracism of dissidents; and the enforcement of speech codes both online and off. "Social justice" has become both a status signifier for the . . . establishment and a tool to discipline the rabble.'[39]

But this harassment, especially in elite universities, is often hypocritical, with staff and students berating political minorities while simultaneously turning a blind eye to other aspects of university life that are morally dubious – such as their university's growing links with the communist regime in China, which despite violating human rights and democratic freedoms has established a strong and growing presence on university campuses across Britain.

Students from China have become an especially important source of money for cash-starved universities in Britain. By the early 2020s, some 27% of all non-EU students studying at UK universities came from China, equivalent to some 152,000 students. Remarkably, this is an increase of 186% on 2011.

In 2023, one study by British think-tank Civitas found that 117 of 140 universities it investigated, or 84% of them, now have significant ties to China, including research partnerships, overseas campuses in China, and PhD programmes that are bankrolled by the Chinese government. Many elite universities, while harassing nonconformist scholars from the West, are more than happy to host 'Confucius Institutes', which are accused of being Chinese state propaganda tools that intimidate Chinese students and monitor what is happening in Western societies.

Understandably, much of this fuels charges of hypocrisy. Consider the University of Cambridge, which has looked into its historic ties with slavery and sought to remove memorials to benefactors because of their supposed links to the slave trade, as well as statues and bells that are linked or any emotionally challenging symbolism. Cambridge has also happily disinvited scholars such as Jordan Peterson, sacked young scholars such as Noah Carl, and urged its students to reflect at length on Britain's involvement with the slave trade.

Yet at the same time, Cambridge has happily accepted tens of millions of pounds' worth of funding in research grants from Chinese corporations such as Huawei, and has a very large Chinese student population, most of whom will be sons and daughters of China's ruling communist elite. A university that seeks to cleanse itself of supposed Western racism and intolerance is simultaneously embracing funding from an openly authoritarian state that is oppressing ethnic minorities and undermining democratic freedoms.

And this breeds other problems. Because Chinese students pay higher international fees, helping universities navigate their intensifying financial crisis, university leaders and administrators are now obsessed with keeping these Chinese students flowing, even if it raises awkward questions about free speech.

In 2024, Michelle Shipworth, an associate professor at University College London with nearly two decades of unblemished service, was banned from teaching a seminar on China to protect the university's financial interests.[40] University administrators stepped in to prevent Shipworth from teaching her course after one Chinese student complained that a discussion about slavery in China had been too 'provocative'. The administrators, remarkably, sided not with the academic but the student, imposing restrictions on Shipworth so that the course remained 'commercially viable' to the lucrative Chinese market.

As universities have become financially dependent on China, in other words, they have become more likely to overlook the negative implications for free speech and academic freedom, often allowing the Chinese Communist Party to deny visas to scholars critical of China, monitor what students say on campus, and contribute to an oppressive climate. They've urged academics to downplay criticism of China and even to turn a blind eye to blatant evidence of cheating by Chinese and other international students.

I experienced this first-hand when I was personally asked not to fail an international student because, in short, our university needed the money. On another occasion I encountered a student from China who, mysteriously, had not said anything in class for about five or six weeks. When I asked him to my office to explore what might be wrong I discovered that he could not speak a word of English – yet here he was, enrolled in an elite Russell Group university in Britain.

While academics fall over themselves to berate the West for being racist, imperialist and oppressive, few if any protest about the growing presence of an oppressive regime on campus which, as Britain's intelligence services make clear, is leaving universities vulnerable. In 2019, MI5 warned universities to put national security ahead of their own commercial interests, telling them that the growing reliance on Chinese money and students was leaving higher education exposed and compromising academic freedom.[41] But few if any have listened.

Confronted with this hypocritical and hostile environment, where the new orthodoxy is prioritized over things that universities used to defend, like free speech and political neutrality, it's not surprising to find that this is also producing another profoundly negative effect on campus: the sheer number of scholars who are 'self-censoring' because, to be blunt, they are too scared to share their views out loud.

'I've lost count of the academics, journalists, teachers, medics and others who have told me they censored themselves to avoid blowing up their jobs and, ultimately, their lives,' wrote gender-critical scholar Helen

Joyce in 2024. 'Yet when I say cancel culture is alive and well on British campuses, I'm told that freedom of speech is not freedom from consequences. It's an amazingly popular line, given its similarity to the words of the Ugandan dictator Idi Amin, who said his opponents had freedom of speech but not freedom after it.'[42]

Again, I've experienced this first-hand, when I 'came out' publicly with my views on Brexit, suggesting the country should respect the result. While this made me a pariah on campus, it also pulled back the curtain to reveal how I was far from alone. Every week, when opening my email, I always had one or two messages from scholars, usually junior colleagues who lacked job security, which made the same point. 'I too supported or accept Brexit,' they would say, 'but I'm scared to share my views because of what this might mean for my career prospects.'

Nor is this self-censorship unique to Britain or Brexit. Alarmingly, across the West, the striking political bias on campus is forcing many academics to conceal their real views. According to one survey of academics in Britain, in 2017, which was conducted by their own trade union, the UCU (which would later deny we have a problem with free speech), more than one in three academics, some 35%, said they were self-censoring, compared to one in five across Europe.[43]

Routinely, it is scholars who do not follow the new

religion who are by far the most likely to hide what they think. Remarkably, according to research by the Center for the Study of Partisanship and Ideology, some 70% of right-leaning scholars feel they are working in campus climates that are hostile towards their beliefs, nine in ten scholars who supported Donald Trump say they do not feel comfortable expressing their views to colleagues, while more than half of all right-wing academics say they are hiding their real views on campus.[44]

I found much the same. When I surveyed scholars working at the world's elite universities, while only one in three who are on the left are hiding their views on campus, more than three-quarters of those on the right are self-censoring in this way.[45]

This simply shows how utterly toxic campuses have become for scholars who are in the political minority, whether they are those who are conservative and supported Brexit or Trump, or those who hold gender-critical views who oppose radical gender ideology. This blatant political discrimination is what much of the wider debate about free speech misses.

In 2018, the BBC's 'Reality Check' asked the following question: is free speech in universities under threat? After sending Freedom of Information requests to every university, it could find only six occasions since 2010 when universities had cancelled speakers and no instances of books being removed or banned. The suggestion, in short, was that this problem was being massively exaggerated.[46]

Yet aside from glossing over the impact of this hostile environment on scholars, this 'Reality Check' also completely ignored the many informal pressures which we have seen are at work on campus, beneath the surface, eroding free expression and silencing alternative viewpoints before any event, debate or reading list has been finalized.

Routinely, because of the strong left-wing bias and groupthink, scholars face below-the-radar pressure not to invite controversial or challenging speakers, not to research areas that might challenge or undermine the new belief system, not to insist that their students be exposed to a diverse range of opinions and beliefs, and not to make a fuss when they are asked by senior academics or diversity, equality and inclusion (DEI) bureaucrats to 'decolonize' their reading lists.

Why would they? In a stifling monoculture where only some views are considered acceptable, doing these things can be tantamount to career suicide. As Helen Joyce reflected after a concerted attempt to have her disinvited from giving a talk at Cambridge, 'When something like this happens to you, you hear from others with similar experiences . . . You will hear about room bookings cancelled, conference invitations rescinded and research papers rejected; about students daubing insults around campus and colleagues whispering behind backs. Individually, the stories range from mundane to heart-rending; collectively, they create a pall of silence.'[47]

This is why investigations like that BBC 'Reality Check' are meaningless, because they ignore what happens upstream of the actual event or scandal. What about all the 'controversial' speakers who were never even invited in the first place? What about all the debates that were never held? What about all the books that are never put into reading lists? And what about all the scholars who are never hired in the first place because they hold different political views?

Ultimately, it was because of these changes, because of what I experienced on campus and witnessed happening to my friends and colleagues at the hands of the so-called 'liberal left', that I found my views beginning to change, and in profound ways.

When it comes to views and perspectives they disagree with, the self-described 'liberals' and 'progressives' who now dominate campus no longer seem all that liberal and progressive to me. On the contrary, they appear just as dogmatic and divisive as the populists they oppose. And when it comes to the universities that I once believed were committed to prioritizing truth, evidence, logic and reason, these institutions no longer appear all that interested in these things.

To me, and many others like me, campus no longer feels like a pleasant, productive and healthy place to be. On the contrary, it appears more interested in promoting political, religious-style dogma over evidence, more interested in promoting a narrow groupthink over genuine debate, more interested in punishing and ostracizing dissenters than allowing a diverse range of viewpoints to flourish.

Increasingly, as I watched all this unfold, I found myself drifting apart from my colleagues, questioning what on earth was happening to higher education. But it wasn't just about how these changes were damaging me and other scholars like me; it was also because of how – more importantly in my eyes – they were also harming our students.

3

Students

I remember the exact moment when I realized that our universities are not just letting down but betraying an entire generation of students.

It was in the aftermath of the shock vote for Brexit, in 2016, when I was still, just about, in charge of our department's 'external speaker programme'. The job description was simple enough: I was responsible for deciding who should be invited on to campus to speak to students. Given that Britain had just voted for Brexit, America had just voted for Donald Trump, and populists were gaining ground across the West, I thought it might be a good idea to let our students hear the kind of arguments that were leading millions of people around the world to reject the expert class and the liberal establishment. After all, I thought, isn't this what university education is supposed to be about – exposing students to the full spectrum of opinions and beliefs that exist in society, even ones they might find uncomfortable and disagreeable?

So I decided to extend an invitation to influential British writer David Goodhart, whose book *The Road to Somewhere* had just set out a compelling argument for why so many people feel so utterly frustrated with the ruling class.[1]

Pointing to Brexit, the rise of Trump and the popularity of politicians such as Marine Le Pen in France, Goodhart drew on a wealth of research in the social sciences to make an important distinction between two groups of people – the people of Somewhere, and the people of Anywhere.

The Anywheres come from the university class. They have undergraduate if not postgraduate degrees, often from the elite universities. They live in the big cities and university towns, come from affluent families, vote for left-wing parties, and put a much stronger emphasis than other people on the importance of things like autonomy, creativity and diversity. They define themselves above all by their 'achieved' identities, such as their educational qualifications and their strongly liberal if not radically progressive beliefs, like those which have come to dominate university campuses.

The people of Somewhere, in sharp contrast, tend not to have passed through university, nor do they come from privileged families. They live outside the cities and university towns, hold more culturally conservative values, and put more of an emphasis on things such as stability, tradition, order, and slowing the pace of social change. They define themselves by their 'ascribed' identities, such as their stronger feelings of attachment to their group, region and nation.

Goodhart's book was a bestseller and established the centre-left former editor of a liberal magazine as one of the most prescient thinkers in Britain. Which is exactly why I invited him on to campus. I wanted our students to hear the same arguments that had recently led 52% of their fellow citizens to vote for Brexit and would later lead many others to vote for Boris Johnson, Nigel Farage and the Reform Party.

I believe such debates are crucial to countering confirmation bias and motivated reasoning, and building more cohesive societies.

But I was not prepared for what followed.

Suddenly, without warning, a special meeting for our *entire* academic department was convened. Nearly thirty full-time members of staff, from senior professors to junior research fellows, were summoned to attend from across the country, at considerable cost to the university.

I had no idea what was going on. But it soon became clear.

'Why has such a controversial speaker been allowed to speak to students without a liberal discussant there to challenge his views?' screamed one of my furious fellow professors. 'Who authorized this?' asked another, joining the moral panic and collective outrage that was now engulfing the meeting.

Others sat there shaking their heads in anger, making it crystal clear to everybody else that they too were just as appalled by what had taken place. It was as if somebody had just asked Kim Jong Un to address our students – though in fairness the North Korean dictator would probably have got a warmer reception than somebody who had voiced sympathy for people who had voted for Brexit.

I sat quietly at the back of the meeting, sliding down into my chair, wondering whether I was working at a serious institution of higher education that was committed to the pursuit of truth through debate and gathering evidence or, instead, some kind of Soviet Gulag that was focused on 're-educating' students in the 'correct' ideology, irrespective of whether it was backed by science.

A few weeks later, as part of the growing backlash against me which I described in the previous chapter, I was removed from my role overseeing the speaker programme. From here on, I was no longer permitted to have any influence over who was invited on to campus to speak to students.

But my confusion didn't end there. Shortly afterwards, the university held another discussion about Brexit, only this time it was between two of Britain's most strident anti-Brexit voices. On one side was our very own university chancellor, former journalist and BBC *Newsnight* presenter Gavin Esler. Like much of the media class, ever since the referendum Esler had morphed into a strident anti-Brexit activist, clearly forgetting that as chancellor of our university he was supposed to represent the views of everybody on campus. On the other side was (Lord) Andrew Adonis, Labour Member of the House of Lords, who was just as strongly opposed to Brexit, believing people should be forced to have a second referendum, presumably so they could make the 'right' decision. There was no pro-Brexit voice in the debate. Nor was there even a neutral voice, somebody who might not have voted for Brexit but accepted the need to respect the democratic vote.

None of my academic colleagues complained. Apparently, they were fine with a completely lopsided debate, so long as it was filled with leftists who shared the groupthink and did not challenge the orthodoxy.

I wandered into the 'debate', watching the two activists complain and criticize, relying more on their opinion than on fact, evidence and logic. And then, as I looked around the room at the students watching on, I suddenly felt an overwhelming sense of sadness and disillusionment.

Is this what our students think higher education is supposed to be about, I wondered? Is this what they are paying all that money for? And is this *really* what universities think is in the best interests of students – hosting debates and creating a campus culture in which there's not actually much debate at all?

Now, you might be reading this and thinking it's just one anecdote from one professor at one university. But it runs much deeper than that. As we'll see in this chapter, my experience at the University of Kent is a symbol of how the stifling new orthodoxy on campus is not just damaging scholars but is now rapidly undermining our students too.

Many people on the right of politics will point to troubling events like the one I just described and say it's evidence of how today's students are being brainwashed by their left-wing, Marxist professors. Seen through this lens, the left-leaning academics who, as we saw in the last chapter, now dominate universities use their positions of influence to spread what Elon Musk and others call the 'woke mind virus'. But this is misleading.

Why? Because what's *really* happening on campus today is that the new ideology is colliding with several other, longer-term factors that have been on the rise in higher education for years, if not decades. And now, this toxic cocktail is lowering academic standards, eroding free speech and academic freedom, and narrowing rather than expanding the minds of our students – which is another reason I decided to leave.

In my experience, one of the most important changes

on campus, which was reflected in the hysteria and moral panic that followed my invitation to David Goodhart, has been the way in which the new ideology has collided with a growing obsession with ensuring that students are not offended and do not experience 'emotional harm'.

Instead of viewing students as young adults who, like diamonds formed under pressure, need to become intellectually resilient and hardened through exposure to different perspectives and rigorous debate, many universities today, especially the elite ones, see them as hyper-fragile, highly sensitive and extremely vulnerable beings who must be coddled.

Two of the first people to notice this worrying trend were Greg Lukianoff and esteemed social psychologist Jonathan Haidt. In a series of essays in the 2010s, which culminated in their book *The Coddling of the American Mind*, published in 2018, they were among the first to explain how and why today's universities are betraying their original purpose and students.

Unlike in the past, they warn, universities have become far more interested in prioritizing the new political goal of 'social justice' over the traditional goal of pursuing truth. In turn, as I learned during the David Goodhart debacle, they have become much more focused on disinviting or cancelling speakers who might in some way jeopardize this openly political project.

Pointing to the rise of terms such as 'microaggressions' – defined as small actions or word choices that are regarded as a kind of violence – and 'trigger warnings' – defined as alerts professors give to students if something might cause them emotional distress – Lukianoff and Haidt argued that these are symbols of a much wider and deeper cultural shift that has been transforming universities over the last fifteen years.

It presumes, they write, 'an extraordinary fragility of the collegiate psyche, and therefore elevates the goal of protecting students from psychological harm. The ultimate aim, it seems, is to turn campuses into "safe spaces" where young adults are shielded from words and ideas that make some uncomfortable. And more than the last, this movement seeks to punish anyone who interferes with that aim, even accidentally.'[2]

But what explains the spread of this hyper-fragility and sensitivity on campus? For Lukianoff and Haidt, part of the answer lies in the more protective parenting style of Baby Boomers who, unlike earlier generations, were less willing to let their children play freely and, in turn, become more resilient.

Children born after 1980 (the Millennials and the Zoomers from Gen-Z), they argue, were more likely than older generations to have their play restricted by their parents, while their schools also became more focused than they were in the past on removing possible dangers in the classroom and playground. Much of this reinforced the message among young people that life is about avoiding rather than managing risks and vulnerabilities, and encouraged them to see the primary role of adults, schools and universities as doing all they can to protect them from emotional and physical harm.

Sociologists Bradley Campbell and Jason Manning have made a similar but much broader argument, suggesting that something even more profound is now playing out across the West. In a similar vein to Lukianoff and Haidt, they argue that many Western nations are now rapidly evolving into an entirely new 'moral culture', and one that is visibly damaging their young people.[3]

Societies used to be organized around a *culture of honour*, in which people responded aggressively to any perceived insult, aggression or challenge so as to uphold their honour in society. They later evolved into a *culture of dignity* where, instead, exercising self-restraint and having a thick skin became a more important marker of one's standing, reflected in the saying 'sticks and stones may break my bones, but words will never hurt me'. But today, in sharp contrast, many Western nations are evolving into a *culture of victimhood*, where, as we see on elite campuses across the West, students and staff have come to view words and speech as 'violence' and are encouraged to respond to any sense that they have suffered 'emotional harm', however slight, by appealing to authorities and confronting the 'aggressor'.

'Victimhood culture,' the authors contend, 'is marked by a low tolerance for slight. It produces a correspondingly low tolerance for all sorts of discomfort and difficulty, even if these are not considered offenses as such. Victimhood culture is also distinguished by a tendency to ask third parties for support in conflicts, and to do so in ways that advertise or exaggerate one's victimization.'[4]

Amid this new moral culture, students have come to expect that those who cause them emotional harm – such as a challenging speaker or scholar – are simply silenced or removed, so as to safeguard the victim and send a message that these acts of 'violence', including the voicing of honest opinion or the tabling of challenging ideas, will not be tolerated.

Furthermore, amid this culture of victimhood students and staff even derive a sense of social status, esteem and honour by portraying themselves as having been 'victimized' in some way, whether at the hands of a speaker who makes them feel uncomfortable or a surrounding structure and society that are 'racist'.

Since 2010, these wider cultural shifts have clearly been reinforced by the rise of social media which, unlike in the past, has made it easier for offended students and scholars to join moral crusades, venting their collective outrage on the likes of Facebook, X and TikTok, and punishing those who are perceived to have caused them emotional harm, such as by unfriending or blocking them, or leading online pile-ons, setting out to destroy the reputation and livelihood of perceived transgressors.

As Lukianoff and Haidt point out, it is telling that the initial wave of students who spent their teenage years on Facebook and social media first began arriving on university campuses around the year 2011, which is exactly when a sharp upsurge of student-led protests, online mobbings of unorthodox scholars and attempted cancellations of scholars and speakers really began to take off. According to the reputable and independent Foundation for Individual Rights and Expression (FIRE), which tracks key trends on campuses in America, between 2000 and 2022 the number of attempts to cancel or sanction scholars exploded, from just four cases in the year 2000 to a record 145 in 2022, most of which were initiated by left-leaning students.[5]

While some Baby Boomers might say university campuses have always been hotbeds of protest and disruption, the very latest studies suggest that, actually, something unique has taken place over the last fifteen years. FIRE finds a dramatic increase in efforts to sanction scholars after 2014, with 81% of all these attempts taking place between the years 2014 and 2022, as online Zoomers, immersed in the new dominant ideology in schools, celebrity culture and social media, came of age and arrived on campus.

It's also worth comparing what's happening today with what happened during the infamous 'Red Scare' era of McCarthyism, in late 1940s and early 1950s America, when fears about supposed communist infiltration became widespread and led to many scholars, scientists and other influential figures being denounced, as covered in the recent *Oppenheimer* film.

Remarkably, at the time of writing, according to data from FIRE, more modern scholars have been sanctioned than during that infamous McCarthy era, while a much larger number of academics today are less willing to share their views. FIRE estimates that whereas 9% of scholars in the McCarthy era were afraid to express their views, in 2022 a much higher 34% felt this way, partly because they were scared about how their increasingly censorious students might respond.

One important symbol of this drift away from facts and logic towards moral outrage and emotion, which is seen by many as the start of the recent cultural revolution on campus, arrived in 2015, when a video of tearful and angry students shrieking in the face of a Yale professor went viral. Why were visibly traumatized students harassing Professor Nicholas Christakis? Because he happened to be master of the college and the husband of fellow academic Erika Christakis, who had questioned whether the school's 'Intercultural Affairs Council' should have asked students to be thoughtful about the 'cultural implications' of their chosen Halloween costumes.

In a carefully crafted email to students and staff, Erika Christakis had dared to ask aloud whether universities were losing their way and instead becoming places where certain views and actions are censored, if not banned. 'Is there no room anymore for a child or young person to be a little bit obnoxious, a little bit inappropriate or provocative or, yes, offensive?' wrote Christakis. 'American universities were once a safe space not only for maturation but also for a certain regressive, or even transgressive, experience; increasingly, it seems, they have become places of censure and prohibition.'

The response from students shocked the country. They protested loudly and aggressively on campus. They demanded that the couple resign or be sacked. And in the shocking video that came to symbolize this new climate of vindictive protectiveness, in which students target those who are perceived to have caused them emotional harm, they shrieked at and harassed Nicholas Christakis.

Eventually, the couple resigned from their positions.

This is not an isolated example. In the years since, many rigorous studies have documented a sharp rise in the number of students who now demand their emotional safety be prioritized over free speech, and who say those who make them feel uncomfortable, including their professors and lecturers, should be silenced and sacked.

In 2023, a study at North Dakota State University, based on a survey of 2,250 students, found that 81% of self-described liberal students said they would report a professor to the authorities if they made comments the students found offensive, compared to a lower but still worrying 53% of conservative students.[6] Astonishingly, more than half of liberal students (51%) said they would report a professor to the authorities who, like Harvard's Roland Fryer in the previous chapter, questioned *on the basis of data* whether there is anti-black bias in police shootings, while almost half of liberal students (some 45%) said they would report a professor who suggested that mandatory Covid vaccinations represented an assault on individual freedom.

As the author of that study, John Bitzan, concluded: 'To me, it's alarming that students are saying, "You can't have an opinion on something that differs from the correct or appropriate opinion without being reported to the university."'

To be honest, when I first read the work of scholars like Lukianoff and Haidt, I thought they must be exaggerating the scale of the problem. Surely, this must be confined to elite campuses in America, I thought, not the more open-minded, gentle, polite world of higher education in Britain.

But then, in the very same year as Lukianoff and Haidt's influential book was published (2018), I watched my own university, the University of Kent, hit the national news when it was revealed the student union wanted to ban fancy-dress costumes that might 'offend' our apparently fragile students. Dressing up as a cowboy, a priest, a nun, a working-class 'chav' or wearing a Mexican sombrero, we were told, was 'offensive, discriminatory, and prejudicial to an individual's race, gender, disability, or sexual orientation, or based on stereotypes'. And nor was my university the only one to exhibit the new obsession with emotional safety.

By 2023, the cultural shift that Lukianoff and Haidt had first pointed to in America had become clearly visible in Britain, too. A major study by the think-tank Civitas found that, much like their counterparts in America, more than 60% of universities in Britain now regularly included references to 'trigger warnings' or 'content notes' to alert their students about emotionally harmful material, while more than half of the 137 universities Civitas examined referenced ideas from the new ideology, such as 'white privilege' and 'anti-racism'.[7]

While my academic colleagues routinely told me the spread of this belief system was being exaggerated by right-wing culture warriors, a growing number of examples from across the country instead suggest the opposite. It has now moved from the margins to the mainstream of university life. These examples include Aberdeen University issuing a trigger warning for *Peter Pan* because students might find it 'emotionally challenging'; students at the University of Chester being warned that reading the Harry Potter books could 'lead to difficult conversations about gender, race, sexuality, class and identity'; Newcastle University warning staff not to use 'patronising or gendered terms, such as girls, pet [a popular Geordie form of address], or ladies'; and Warwick banning the term 'trigger warnings' because it might 'upset students'.

In 2021, I also experienced this first-hand when another moment in my journey towards leaving university life arrived. Once again Kent hit the national news when it was revealed it was making students take a compulsory 'diversity' test. Aside from including references to 'microaggressions' and 'gender pronouns', students were forced to complete a 'white privilege quiz', in which they had to identify the alleged benefits that only white people enjoy.

Examples of this supposed 'white privilege' included wearing second-hand clothes 'without having people attribute these choices to the bad morals, the poverty, or the illiteracy of my race', 'going shopping without being followed or harassed', having 'neutral or pleasant neighbours', and 'doing well in challenging situations without being called a credit to my race'. With absolutely no evidence presented to support these claims, students were nonetheless informed that 'systemic racism is built into the very building blocks of British society', including schools, courts and churches, and that even people from minority backgrounds engage in so-called 'white ideology', so that they might benefit from the supposed power 'whiteness' brings.

It was yet more evidence of how universities were pushing highly dubious and unscientific concepts like 'white privilege' and 'systemic racism' on to their students, treating these ideas as though they are fact when in reality they are highly contested beliefs that need to be tested and scrutinized through empirical research and healthy debate – debate that no longer takes place on campus.

And this is the case not just in the less prestigious universities, like Kent, but in the top educational institutions in the country, which produce the vast majority of politicians, CEOs and leaders.

As Civitas also found, more than 80% of Britain's elite universities, including Oxford and Cambridge, now routinely use trigger warnings in their material, compared to 46% of non-elite universities. The country's elite universities, moreover, are especially likely to immerse students in concepts from the key academic theories that underpin the new ideology, like postcolonial theory, critical race theory and gender ideology, teaching them about 'white privilege' and a more aggressive brand of 'anti-racism', which essentially demands discrimination in the name of anti-discrimination, encouraging people to discriminate against whites or straight people in the name of protecting minorities.

For Lukianoff and Haidt, this reflects how today's universities are losing sight of their purpose. Instead of remaining politically independent, focused on truth, and encouraging students to become critical thinkers, many are forcing students to embrace an openly political, divisive and corrosive brand of identity politics which is pushing them to see privilege and oppression in every social interaction while also becoming more intolerant of others. Seen through this warped lens, they write, 'Life is a battle between good people and bad people. Furthermore, there is no escaping the conclusion as to who the evil people are. The main axes of oppression usually point to one intersectional address: straight white males.'

This became impossible to ignore after 7 October 2023, when Hamas terrorists committed atrocities in Israel. In the weeks and months that followed, one major survey after another found that university students were consistently the most likely to voice strong opposition to Israel, support for Hamas, and to say that terrorist acts committed by minorities (Palestinians) against an oppressive majority (Israel) could be 'justified'. In 2023, in America, some 48% of all Zoomers – so, the under-twenty-five age group – said they sided more with Hamas than Israel, a view only 16% of Americans shared. Zoomers were also the only generation to lend majority support to the idea that 'the Hamas killing of 1,200 Israeli civilians can be justified'.[8] In Britain, too, Zoomers were the least likely to say they sympathized more with Israel than Palestine, the most likely to say they openly supported Palestinians, and the least likely to view Hamas as a terrorist group.[9]

What this reflects is the sheer extent to which today's students are being pushed to embrace the new ideology, in which Jews and white majorities are seen as dangerous oppressors, dominating, and discriminating against people of colour, while people from minority groups, even ones that commit mass murder and rape, are seen as inherently superior and virtuous. Through things like post-colonial theory and its obsession with 'decolonization', which we will explore more fully in the next chapter, students are being encouraged to view Western nations as inherently 'racist' and their national identities and history as a source of shame.

In Britain, in 2022, one study by the think-tank Policy Exchange found that while most British adults reject the suggestion that Britain was founded on racism and remains 'structurally racist', young Zoomers from Gen-Z, born from the late 1990s onward, were the only group to voice more support for than opposition to this claim.

Reflecting how such beliefs are now circulating widely in not just higher education but also primary and secondary schools, the same study found that nearly 60% of Britain's Zoomers have been taught concepts such as 'white privilege', 'systemic racism' and 'unconscious bias' at school – more evidence of how these ideas have moved from the margins to the mainstream.[10]

Many of these ideas are not supported by evidence, like the claim, which you hear often on campus, that the education system is 'structurally racist' and biased against minorities and so, as a result, universities must invest heavily in trying to recruit more students from minority backgrounds. While this is admirable, the reality is that it's children from the white working class, not children from minority backgrounds, who are routinely left behind and overlooked at every level of the education system.[11]

I first pointed this out in 2022 while giving evidence to the House of Commons Select Committee on Education. For the first time in history, I said, a lower share of white British schoolchildren now go to the elite universities than children from any other ethnic group in the country. While 41% of British Chinese students progress into the most prestigious universities, and 16% of British Asians and 11% of black British students, only 10.5% of white British children follow them into these institutions.[12]

As usual, I was attacked on social media by academics who suggested I was 'racist' for pointing this out. But the reality is that while university leaders now fall over themselves to talk about how they are making their institutions more diverse and equitable, they show little if any interest in the very children who are most likely to be left behind: children from the white majority.

Influenced by the new ideology, universities would rather indulge in a performative and tokenistic brand of virtue signalling, prioritizing children from minority backgrounds while also focusing heavily on recruiting students from authoritarian regimes such as China who, to be blunt, pay more money.

Look, for example, at the proliferation of scholarships for children from minority backgrounds which are not made available to children from the white majority, such as the Amos Bursary for students of African and Caribbean descent, the Bank of England Black Future Leaders Sponsorship Programme for students of black or mixed background, the Black Academic Futures programme at the University of Oxford, which awards fifty scholarships to students from black and mixed backgrounds, the Black Bristol Scholarship Programme, and the Diversity100 PhD studentship programme at Birkbeck, University of London, which is for prospective or current PhD students who are from ethnic minorities, among many others.

Unfortunately, nowhere near the same amount of effort is devoted to helping children who are actually the most likely to be left behind. In 2019, the National Education Opportunities Network pointed out that fewer than one in five of Britain's universities have targets for poor white students, despite the fact they are less likely to go to university than Asian and black teenagers.[13]

While today's students are routinely immersed in these misleading claims and encouraged to adopt a corrosive brand of identity politics, the new obsession with protecting their 'emotional safety', victimhood, and punishing would-be transgressors is breeding a wider intolerance.

In Britain, much like America, recent research suggests that students are noticeably more intolerant than they used to be. Between 2016 and 2022, the Higher Education Policy Institute found that the share of students who think that a professor should be fired if they teach material that offends students more than doubled, surging from 15% to 36%.[14] The same study also found that, since 2016, students have become more supportive of a range of other things which reflect the creeping influence of the new belief system on campus. Support for trigger warnings has surged by twenty points to 86%. Support for removing offensive memorials is up twenty-five points to 76%. Support for creating 'safe spaces' for students is up fourteen points to 62%. And support for the suggestion that students who feel threatened 'should always have their demands for safety respected' is up eleven points to 79%. Clearly, this isn't all to do with intolerance of people who hold different views, but these findings do suggest a heightened sense of fragility and more preoccupation with emotional safetyism than in the past.

Today's students, the study found, have also become more supportive than they used to be of banning political groups from speaking at universities, of thinking authorities should consult special interest groups on campus such as religious and gender societies before organizing events for students, of stopping events from happening or disrupting them, of 'no-platforming' controversial speakers, of thinking the student union should ban 'offensive' speakers, of giving their professors mandatory training on understanding other cultures, and of removing memorials and statues on campus that might offend them. The study's conclusion? That compared to only a few years earlier, students 'have become significantly less supportive of free expression'.[15]

The key point is that, under the influence of the new ideology, when today's students think that central aspects of liberalism such as free speech, free expression and academic freedom conflict with the political goals of promoting 'equality and diversity' on campus and protecting their emotional safety, they are much more likely than older generations to say they're willing to sacrifice the former in the name of the latter – which is why the new ideology is so damaging.

According to the Higher Education Policy Institute,

for example, when students were asked to choose between ensuring that all students are protected from discrimination or, instead, ensuring that universities allow free speech, students leaned 61% to 37% in favour of prioritizing protecting students from discrimination over protecting free speech.

In 2022, similarly, researchers at King's College London asked the British public and university students whether people should be able to say what they want or be careful not to offend others. Consistently, on a wide range of issues that have forced their way into our political debates – Brexit, climate change, Britain's empire, religion, immigration, refugees, gender identity, transgender issues, sexuality, and racism – today's students are much *less* likely than the public to think people should be free to say what they want, and much *more* likely to say people should be careful not to offend others.[16]

And there are good reasons to think this challenge will only get stronger, not weaker, in the years ahead.

In recent years, among the expert class, it's become fashionable to argue that the West has finally reached 'peak woke', that the new ideology has climaxed and will now steadily fade from view as people become more wary of and exhausted by cancel culture, political correctness and the culture wars. But one only has to look at the latest research on what is happening on campus among young students and younger academics to see how misleading this narrative is. Far from peaking, the research suggests this belief system is only becoming stronger and more widespread among Gen-Z.

In the universities, younger scholars and PhD students, who will soon become the professors of tomorrow, are significantly less tolerant than their older colleagues of people who hold different political views.

In 2021, the Center for the Study of Partisanship and Ideology found that a striking 43% of PhD students in America would support dismissing a fellow scholar whose research suggested that 'diversity' has negative effects on a society, while an astonishing 82% of students openly said they would discriminate in some way or another against a right-wing scholar.[17] More than two-thirds of younger scholars, furthermore, said that instead of remaining neutral when deciding who to appoint to an academic job they would favour a supporter of Bernie Sanders over a supporter of Donald Trump. In short, younger scholars (under thirty-five) are about twice as likely as older scholars (over fifty) to voice their support for cancel culture and restricting free speech on campus in the name of protecting others from emotional harm.

And this is especially the case for young university-educated women who in recent years have moved sharply to the cultural left and become noticeably less supportive of free speech, compared to their male counterparts. In 2024, *The Economist* pointed out how, over the last twenty years, young women have become much more liberal than young men.[18] In Britain, for example, a plurality of women aged twenty-five or younger believe J. K. Rowling should be dropped by her publisher for her gender-critical views, for rejecting the suggestion that gender identity should supersede biological sex. They are more likely than young men and also older women to think this way.[19]

And in their comprehensive review of evidence in the social sciences published in *Quillette Magazine*, academics Cory Clark and Bo Winegard point to similarly striking trends among younger women.[20] For a start, they note (and applaud) the fact that women have become more prominent in the university class, outpacing men at every level of the education system, including becoming more likely than men to receive doctoral degrees. This means they are playing a more influential role in the universities than in the past and will play an even more influential role in the future. But at the same time, women also have different traits, tendencies and priorities that will continue to change the nature and direction of universities.

As Clark and Winegard point out, compared to men, they are significantly more likely to endorse a range of policies and positions that will support, if not spread, the new ideology in the years ahead.

Summarizing the evidence, the authors note how women are significantly more supportive of the idea that universities should work to protect students from offensive ideas, are more opposed to allowing controversial speakers to speak on campus, are more likely to support dismissal campaigns against scholars whose research reaches a 'controversial' conclusion, are more supportive of disinviting speakers if students threaten to protest, are more likely to support a 'confidential reporting system' at universities which students can use to report offensive comments made by other students or staff, and are more likely to think that stories in student newspapers which touch on controversial issues should require approval from university administrators.

And that's not all. When presented with a trade-off between prioritizing issues that are central to the new belief system on campus or, instead, defending free speech and free expression, women are especially likely to endorse the former. Compared to men, they are much more likely to think that meeting 'diversity quotas' on university reading lists is more important than ensuring students are exposed to 'intellectually foundational' texts.

While men are more likely to think protecting free speech is more important than promoting a more inclusive society, women are more likely to think the opposite – that promoting an inclusive society is more important than protecting free speech. And while most men think it's never acceptable to shout down speakers or to try to prevent them from delivering their remarks, most women think this is sometimes or always acceptable. Consistently, the authors note, in a wide range of studies, men are more likely to want to prioritize things such as academic freedom and advancing knowledge while women are more likely to want to prioritize 'social justice' and the emotional wellbeing of others.

The overall theme of these differences is that men are more committed than women to the pursuit of truth as the *raison d'être* of science, while women are more committed to various moral goals, such as equity, inclusion, and the protection of vulnerable groups. Consequently, men are more tolerant of controversial and potentially offensive scientific findings being pursued, disseminated, and discussed, and women are more willing to obstruct or suppress science perceived to be potentially harmful or offensive. Put more simply, men are relatively more interested in advancing what is *empirically correct*, and women are relatively more interested in advancing what is *morally desirable*.[21]

As Zoomers continue to leave campus and enter the world – in other words, entering graduate trainee schemes, corporations, the media, and the creative and cultural industries – they will likely continue to impose on other institutions the belief system that now dominates campuses. And this appears especially likely to be the case with young women.

Back in the universities, meanwhile, like those scholars we met in the last chapter, students who hold a different outlook are now often finding themselves shut down and silenced, forced to self-censor. This is another damaging effect of the ideology on campus, pushing not just renegade academics and professors to keep their views hidden but an alarmingly large number of students too.

Today, an astonishingly high number of students in Western universities openly admit they are hiding their real views or avoiding certain subjects for fear of saying the wrong thing, in the very institutions that are supposed to encourage them to speak openly and without fear.

In America, in 2023, the Heterodox Academy Campus Expression Survey found that nearly half of all students, 47%, are reluctant to discuss issues such as the Israel–Palestine conflict, while 45% are reluctant to discuss politics, 42% feel the same way about trans issues, and 33% say the same about abortion.[22] In fact, nearly 80% of students are reluctant to discuss, ask questions about or share their ideas about at least one of these 'controversial' topics, which is not exactly a ringing endorsement of institutions that are supposed to encourage students to debate their way around thorny social issues.

And there are enormous differences by political affiliation. As the American College Student Freedom, Progress and Flourishing Survey, released in 2021, found, while some 43% of students said they no longer feel comfortable 'sharing controversial opinions in class', conservative students were much more likely than their liberal peers to feel this way, which again reflects the negative effects of the strong left-wing bias on campus.[23] Whereas most liberal students, some 66%, felt comfortable sharing their views about a controversial or sensitive topic in class, most conservative students, some 58%, felt uncomfortable.

The same study also found big differences in the extent to which students from across the political landscape think their professors are creating a climate in which people who hold different views feel comfortable sharing those views with others – something that should be standard in higher education. Yet, again, while 90% of liberal students think their professors create a welcoming climate for people with diverse views, only 56% of conservative students feel the same way, reflecting once again how students who do not share the dominant views on campus feel more marginalized in the classroom.

In Britain, too, an alarmingly large number of students now say they are deliberately remaining silent in class because they fear what might happen to their career prospects and friendship groups if they say the wrong thing. In 2023, Bobby Duffy and his team at King's College London looked into what was happening on campus and found, shockingly, that more than two-thirds of all students, some 67%, refrain from sharing their views about controversial issues such as religion, race, immigration and animal rights.[24] While academics and administrators line up on social media to claim there is no problem on campus, more than half their students (51%) now agree with the statement 'The climate at my university prevents some people from saying things they believe because others might find them offensive'.

It wasn't always like this.

Historian Niall Ferguson has recalled how the climate on campus has changed over the last forty years. In an earlier era, he writes, there was a general agreement that the central purpose of a university was the pursuit of truth and that the crucial means to that end were freedom of conscience, thought, speech and publication. 'Those of us who were fortunate to be undergraduates in the 1980s remember the exhilarating combination of intellectual freedom and ambition to which all this gave rise. Yet, in the past decade, exhilaration has been replaced by suffocation, to the point that I feel genuinely sorry for today's undergraduates.'[25]

He has a point. Look around any campus today and it'll be hard to find the same sense of exhilaration. Nearly half of all students, some 48%, told those researchers at King's College London that their universities had become less tolerant of a wide range of viewpoints. And right-leaning students were especially likely to think so, with 78% of Brexit supporters and 65% of Conservative students thinking universities had become much less tolerant of people with different views, compared to only 43% of Remainers and 37% of Labour-supporting students.[26] As professors have moved sharply to the left, in other words, and as a groupthink has taken hold of campus, they have left many students, especially conservative ones, feeling unable to speak openly in class.

Some might respond to this by saying, well, only a minority of students feel unable to share their views, so what's the problem? But as Cambridge scholar Arif Ahmed points out, free speech is, and always has been, a counter-majoritarian principle.[27] It's there to protect minorities and ensure their voice is heard. Saying there is no problem if only a small minority of students are self-censoring is like saying there is no problem with poor healthcare because it only affects a few sick people.

Promoting and protecting certain views at the expense of others is a dangerous practice, and shutting down or discouraging free debate can have profound consequences. One example took place within the National Health Service when, twenty years ago, a few brave whistle-blowers went against the grain by pointing to medical outrages that were being perpetrated against children in Britain's gender clinics, arguing that there was insufficient evidence to encourage them to undergo 'gender transition'.

Many of these individuals at the time were harassed, bullied and shut down by radical pro-trans activists, who found their way into influential administrative positions and then used this power to silence those they disagreed with. It was not until 2024, after a few of these whistle-blowers spoke out again, and then Dr Hilary Cass published her major review into NHS child gender medicine, that things began to change. Not only was there insufficient evidence to be pushing children down medical pathways, such as on to drugs like puberty blockers, warned Cass, but many people in healthcare, like many people in the universities, were also in the grip of a dangerous groupthink that was intolerant of different perspectives.

'I have faced criticism,' wrote Dr Cass, 'for engaging with groups and individuals who take a social just-ice approach and advocate for gender affirmation . . . The knowledge and expertise of experienced clini-cians who have reached different conclusions about the best approach to care are sometimes dismissed and invalidated.'

As on campus, when confronted with a radical activist minority, many people in the National Health Service simply became unable to speak openly. 'There are few other areas of healthcare where professionals are so afraid to openly discuss their views,' wrote Cass, 'where people are vilified on social media, and where name-calling echoes the worst bullying behaviour.'[28]

It's another example of what happens when a group-think crowds out free speech and free expression. Had there been a healthy debate which respected and represented a diverse range of perspectives, then the influence of a minority of radical activists would have been diluted and, most importantly, fewer children would have suffered irrevocable damage, having been pushed into medical procedures for which there was insufficient evidence.

Back on campus, in my own experience, many students are clearly aware of how this groupthink is eroding debate and leaving them poorly prepared for what awaits them after university.

I always encountered this two or three weeks into the start of a new term when, like clockwork, the same thing would happen. After gaining enough confidence to come and speak to me, a handful of students would approach and say something like 'I've been waiting to take your course because until now I feel like I've been given a biased view'. I became known on campus, in other words, as one of the only professors who openly challenged the dominant groupthink. But why?

More than a few students, it was clear, looked at their professors and lecturers, at their carefully crafted reading lists and events, and could see the blatant left-wing bias. And whenever I asked them why they went along with it, why they didn't complain, they would usually say something like: 'I'm just here to get a first-class degree. I don't want to cause any problems.'

I found it all very depressing. Here were bright young students, enrolling in university because they wanted to broaden their horizon and get stuck into thorny debates, only then to discover that many of the people teaching them had no interest in doing this at all.

As I've seen first-hand in Britain, these changes, the damaging effects of the ideology, are being exacerbated by another negative change on campus, which is the growing obsession among higher education regulators, politicians and university leaders with a new way of measuring the so-called 'success' of universities – something called 'student satisfaction'.

What matters on campus, increasingly, is not maintaining academic rigour, high intellectual standards and developing well-rounded, critical thinkers who have been exposed to a diverse range of views. No, what really matters is ensuring that fee-paying students, who are now viewed as consumers, remain fully 'satisfied' with their university experience, are having a 'good time', and are certainly not experiencing anything that might jeopardize this, such as having their emotional safety triggered or being presented with a speaker they don't like.

This was one of the most shocking developments during my time on campus. Increasingly, academics have watched students rather than themselves accumulate more and more power, leaving students with the impression they should have the right to decide what they are taught, how they are taught, and by whom. This, too, is undermining standards in higher education, putting students in charge of what they are willing to learn rather than actual experts determining what they need to learn.

Far from some fringe administrative exercise, student satisfaction scores have now become a key measure of how universities are evaluated, with the National Student Survey in Britain, first launched in 2005, rating universities in a league table based on how satisfied their students feel. While some of the questions in this survey are useful, probing student perceptions about the quality of teaching and campus facilities, what it ultimately reflects is how universities are now often run by commercial needs rather than an overriding sense of mission, while their students are treated more like consumers than intrepid intellectual explorers, with their likes, dislikes and particular concerns now guiding the direction of higher education.

In turn, maintaining high intellectual standards, free speech and the like are downgraded in favour of prioritizing the perceived emotional wellbeing and happiness of students on campus, with administrators often worrying that if students do experience 'emotional harm' they might complain and lower the university's position in the national league tables which potential future students use to decide which university to attend.

One example of how this clashes with aspects that are more important to higher education, such as free speech and debate, is what happened in 2022 when gender-critical writer Helen Joyce was invited to speak to students at the University of Cambridge on the subject of 'criticising gender-identity ideology: what happens when speech is silenced'. Given that Joyce is openly critical of radical gender ideology, it was unsurprising that Cambridge's students protested against her looming arrival. But what was much more surprising was the reaction of their professors, who in theory are supposed to be in favour of exposing their students to a range of viewpoints.

Remarkably, as the debate approached, a senior professor and master of the college, Pippa Rogerson, emailed students and staff rebuking her own academic staff for hosting the debate with Joyce. Rogerson described Joyce as 'offensive, insulting and hateful'. She also forbade the academic who had invited her from publicizing the event on university email lists and then tried to disrupt the event at the last moment by demanding that it be ticketed. While Rogerson did stress in her letter to staff and students that free speech is a fundamental principle, she also argued that 'on some issues which affect our community we cannot stay neutral', that the debate did not contribute to 'an inclusive and welcoming home for our students', and made it clear that neither she nor other senior members of staff would attend the event.

For students who felt emotionally challenged by the debate, meanwhile, a 'safe space' welfare tearoom was made available, to help them process the 'understandable hurt and anger' that was caused by inviting Joyce.[29]

Universities have been transformed into private-sector-style corporations that charge hefty tuition fees, so students have been transformed into consumers and are now treated as such. Like any large successful corporation, from McDonald's to Coca-Cola, universities now work overtime to ensure that their consumers are kept happy, keep spending their money, and do not endure any adverse experiences. After all, the customer is always right.

As Professor Frank Furedi, an expert in the so-called 'culture wars', pointed out, this has created a climate in which universities are utterly obsessed with avoiding complaints, fearful that any dispute with their fee-paying customers (read: students) could lead to legal problems. In turn, this is cultivating what he calls 'defensive education', which is completely focused on minimizing any potential source of student unrest, which would rather flatter than challenge fee-paying students.

So professors like me are now actively discouraged from exercising our professional judgement, such as when offering feedback to students, responding to student complaints, or querying whether a student has cheated. If the entire incentive structure in the university is to keep students happy, to ensure they give us high scores in student satisfaction surveys, then why would you cause a stink on campus by demanding that students work harder, by failing their essays, or by suggesting they are cheating?

And this is feeding into the wider political crisis on campus. As Noah Carl (that young researcher who was sacked by Cambridge after emotionally challenged students protested) notes, while the strong left-wing bias on campus and the rise of groupthink is eroding free speech and academic freedom, so too are these wider administrative changes. 'Admittedly,' he writes, 'the academy's left-liberal skew is probably not the only factor behind the rise of free speech restrictions and political correctness at universities. Another likely explanation is the increase in university tuition, which has occurred both in Britain and the United States. Because they now have to pay hefty fees upfront, students are increasingly treated like consumers, rather than prospective scholars, so that when they demand restrictions on free speech, universities supply those restrictions accordingly.'[30]

The never-ending quest to satisfy students also helps to explain why universities routinely rush to align themselves with liberal progressive moral crusades and campaigns which appear to reflect the interests and priorities of their students, like joining the moral panic on campus after the death of George Floyd and rushing to pledge allegiance to Black Lives Matter. Increasingly, this obsession with student satisfaction is leading universities to abandon their role as politically independent institutions that are solely focused on the search for truth and instead morph into openly political activist entities that now clearly see their role in society as taking sides with their students, most notably in the so-called 'culture wars', fearful that if they don't closely align their cultural values then they might upset the liberal progressive sensibilities of their fee-paying customers.

And this is arguably having many other insidious effects, such as contributing to the remarkable grade inflation that has been taking place in recent years. Given that many universities are now on the brink of financial ruin and have also been reshaped around things like student satisfaction scores, is it really any wonder that the number of students who are now receiving first-class degrees has shot through the roof?

Once a highly prestigious indicator of intellectual

ability, today first-class degrees are commonplace, making it impossible for employers to distinguish between candidates. In 2010 in Britain, for example, 16% of students graduated with first-class degrees; by the early 2020s it had rocketed to 40%. And in 2024, astonishingly, the regulator Office for Students concluded that nearly half of all first-class degrees awarded to students could not be justified, given the previous attainment of students and other factors, while nearly one in four students who were awarded three D grades at A-level went on to get a first-class degree at university![31]

One example of how the obsession with student satisfaction is driving up grades and lowering standards happened at the University of Sheffield in 2019. As Harry Lambert at the *New Statesman* documented in a piece called 'The Great University Con', when students complained about their marks for an end-of-year essay the head of department quickly sent them an email thanking them for their patience and apologizing for 'normal procedures' failing them. The department promptly decided to 'uplift' all marks, with the most poorly performing students having theirs raised by nearly 40%. 'Again, our apologies,' they went on, 'but we hope that this is a satisfactory resolution.'[32]

As Lambert rightly notes, what happened at Sheffield was not unique but merely one part in a wider story: the great university con. Over the past three decades, successive governments on both the left and right have been imposing a set of perverse incentives on universities, the effect of which has been to degrade and devalue the quality of university degrees. 'Academic standards have collapsed,' he goes on. 'In many institutions, it is the students who now educate the universities, in what grades they will tolerate and how much work they are willing to do.'

In 2022, this time in America, another shocking example of this arrived when an esteemed professor of organic chemistry was disciplined by New York University after more than eighty students signed a petition complaining that his class was too hard, and they were receiving low marks. As usual, the case was not dealt with by academics who specialized in the course material but one of a growing number of university administrators who are not specialists and are incapable of deciding whether or not the standards are too high or too low. Remarkably, they even refused to allow the professor to see the students' petition, before firing him.

The professor, Maitland Jones Jr, who had previously taught at the elite Princeton University for forty years, made no secret of the fact that he saw this as a symbol of wider changes he has observed on campus over this time. Students, he noted, were no longer coming to class as often. They were not engaging as much with his course content. They increasingly accused professors of being insufficiently sensitive to the fashionable issues of the day. They increasingly demanded 'accommodations', such as online multiple-choice exams. And universities, he warned, were now 'coddling students' rather than respecting their judgement or that of their highly trained professors.

'What is overwhelmingly important,' he went on, 'is the chilling effect of such intervention by administrators on teaching overall and especially on untenured professors. Can a young assistant professor, almost all of whom are not protected by tenure, teach demanding material? Dare they give real grades? Their entire careers are at the peril of complaining students and deans who seem willing to turn students into nothing more than tuition-paying clients.'[33]

In my experience, these problems became especially visible during the Covid-19 pandemic, when universities lowered standards even more by adopting 'no detriment' policies to ensure their students were not adversely affected. While the case for doing so was justifiable during the most acute phase of the pandemic, the problem is that many of the more lenient policies were then kept in place for much longer than necessary.

I was told to be much more flexible with students, to no longer monitor their attendance, to give them longer deadlines, to move to 'open book' exams and use resources like 'online quizzes', which they complete at home where it's impossible for professors like me to know who is doing the work.

The Covid pandemic and the obsession with student satisfaction have also encouraged something else which is having a damaging impact on students: the rise of 'remote' learning, where university courses are moved online rather than being taught in traditional 'face-to-face' lectures and seminars. Instead of students spending time on campus, immersed in an intellectually vibrant climate while developing their interpersonal skills through face-to-face contact with professors and students, they are now encouraged to watch their course content online, away from campus, alone in their rooms. The Netflix generation, the generation of Zoomers who have become used to binge-watching entire seasons of television shows in just a few days or even a few hours, can now sit at home doing exactly the same with their university course, binge-watching lectures in just a few hours.

Increasingly, universities are adopting 'blended learning' or 'hybrid learning', where classes are delivered simultaneously online and offline, allowing students to choose whether they attend in person. Unsurprisingly, many choose not to.

When I began teaching in the universities, in the early 2000s, students who missed class two weeks in a row were usually contacted by administrators. Sometimes we even sent letters to their home address so that their parents were made aware. But in more recent years things changed dramatically. When I was told to record my lectures and put them online – 'because that's what the students want' – attendance collapsed. And nobody was really monitoring attendance anyway. I went from teaching in vibrant lecture halls where students and professors got to know one another to teaching in cold, depressing, half-empty rooms where the few students who bothered to turn up looked just as disillusioned as me. 'Is this what university is supposed to look and feel like?' I could see them wondering.

It's a fair question. In 2024, in Britain, one report found that nearly half of all students say they feel lonely at university, nearly half say they are less engaged with university activities than they expected to be, while one in four said they had never engaged with these activities at all.[34]

Even students are beginning to realize these changes are not in their interest. Despite student satisfaction becoming central to the university experience, a culture of complaining has become embedded within the higher education experience.

In 2022, the Higher Education Policy Institute reported that only 35% of students thought they were getting good value for money from their university. Complaints hit a record high, with many students concerned about how their courses were being delivered, the lack of in-person facilities, and farming out teaching from experienced university professors to junior PhD students who are not trained lecturers.

At the same time, many students are just gaming the system. Because they are no longer required to attend everything, including seminars and lectures, students will often only watch, say, three or four weeks' worth of the course content, enough to cover their chosen essay topic and leave them prepared to cover two or three questions on the exam, while the rest of the course content will simply be ignored.

I used to see this every term, because I could monitor how often students engaged with their course content online. I could see when they logged in, how long they stayed, and how often they returned. What happened? Well, like clockwork, there was no activity at all for the first few weeks with quiet lectures and half-empty seminar rooms. And then, as the deadlines for essays approached, there was a sudden rush of activity as everybody began to binge-watch their course content in the final two or three weeks. How is that encouraging the reflection, contemplation or critical thinking that were once considered essential to higher education?

And the shift to online teaching is exacerbating other problems, such as plagiarism and cheating. At a recent conference, university experts warned that the growing use of online teaching is making it easier for students to essentially cheat their way through their degrees, whether by taking exams at home, with materials and books available, using AI software, or relying on 'essay mills', where they simply buy essays that have been written by other people elsewhere in the world. And because professors like me no longer really know their students, because they are never really around them any more, it's become almost impossible for them to spot when this is happening.

While they'll never say it out loud, many professors and academics support the move to online learning because, to be blunt, it means they don't have to go to campus, can avoid their students, and can work from home. University administrators, meanwhile, support it because it means they can recruit more students than their already overcrowded lecture halls and campuses can hold, while also selling courses to lucrative overseas markets.

But for the students and their families who expect university to be an intellectually enriching, immersive, stimulating experience, these changes have been very damaging and have eroded public confidence.

What really matters, then, in my view at least, is how the rise of the new ideology has been colliding with these wider cultural and administrative changes to undermine the quality of higher education for students. We are sending record numbers of students into our universities but at the same time these institutions are prioritizing their emotional safety over free speech, academic standards and the need to expose them to a diverse range of views. This is delivering, fundamentally, a bad education, leaving them poorly prepared for the world that awaits them off campus.

And, unfortunately, the problems do not end there. Because this new version of university life is not only damaging scholars and students, it is also being reinforced by the wider 'system' of higher education that surrounds and cultivates what is now taking place on campus.

4

System

The decision to quit my professorship was shaped not only by what I have witnessed happening to scholars and students; it was also influenced by what I've seen happen to the surrounding system of higher education.

What do I mean by the word 'system'? I'm referring to an increasingly vast and powerful bureaucracy that claims to speak on behalf of universities, their staff and students but which is now, in my view, robbing them of a rich and balanced education.

This system comprises an assortment of university vice-chancellors, senior bureaucrats and administrators, unelected higher education agencies, think-tanks, research councils, charities and lobbying groups, all of which have been accumulating more power and influence, which they are using to impose and entrench the new dominant set of values from above, in top-down fashion.

Together, they are fundamentally corrupting the universities' traditional *raison d'être*, viewing them not

as institutions that should pursue reason and knowledge but, instead, as vehicles they can use to pursue
and promote an openly political agenda – to divide
different groups on the basis of their identities, to prioritize dogma over evidence and scientific knowledge,
to impose new speech restrictions, and to try to convince
students and staff they are living in institutionally racist
societies. This is not to say that any single figure, organization, or research council is driving all this but rather
to suggest that, overall, the system of higher education
is steadily being politicized and led away from the traditional goals of the universities.

While a radical minority of activist scholars are promoting these changes for ideological reasons because
they genuinely believe in them, today they've formed
an unofficial alliance of sorts with a rapidly expanding
army of higher education bureaucrats who, because of
how this bureaucracy has grown and been politicized,
are now incentivized to strengthen and spread the new
worldview for very different reasons – usually because
they owe their jobs, salaries, livelihoods and sense of
social status and esteem on campus to doing exactly this.

One person who has tracked these changes more
than most is Professor Doug Stokes. He refers to this
alliance between university bureaucrats, activist scholars, unelected 'equalities' organizations and charities
and research councils as the 'grievance industrial complex', because whether for ideological or administrative

reasons they all have a vested interest in amplifying grievances and identity politics to try and bring about sweeping, radical change on campus.[1]

I've had a first-row seat for this revolution within the system of higher education. For twenty years I've watched these activists and administrators move to hard-wire the new ideology into every facet of university life – reading lists for students, official guidance for academics, applications for research jobs and grants, admissions policies, and compulsory training. And at the heart of it all is a very different and very radical idea of what the university should be about.

Unlike what we might call the 'traditional liberal vision' which views universities as institutions that pursue truth through a commitment to free speech, academic freedom and meritocracy, all while treating people equally, the system of higher education is now advocating and promoting a very different vision of these institutions.

Increasingly, it views universities as vehicles that can be used to pursue and promote political goals, such as redistributing power and resources from majorities to minorities, prioritizing equal outcomes over equality of opportunity, incubating students in anti-Western 'revisionist' ideas and upholding unscientific beliefs, treating staff and students unequally on the basis of their racial, sexual or gender identities, and imposing restrictions on speech and language in the name of protecting people from emotional harm.

These changes really do matter. They matter not only because they show how this system – the 'water in which the fish swim' – is being radically transformed but because they also show us how the people who work in this system would like to see Western societies more generally.

Instead of viewing campuses as politically neutral environments, many see them instead as a microcosm of how they would eventually like the West to look – a place where free enterprise, free markets, free speech, individual rights and the equal treatment of groups are replaced by something else entirely.

It's impossible to make sense of how this system has been transformed without first making sense of how it has ballooned in size. We have already seen, in chapter 2, how academics have moved sharply to the left over the last fifty years. At the same time, the bureaucracy that surrounds them has also massively expanded. Both of these changes are critical to making sense of how the universities have come unstuck.

Beginning in America, between 1976 and 2018, the number of full-time university administrators and other 'professional' staff rocketed by 164% and 452%, respectively. But at the same time the number of full-time academics increased by only 92%, and student enrolment increased by only 78%.[2] The rapid growth of the university bureaucracy, in other words, has outpaced the growth of the academic and student population. In many of America's leading universities and colleges, it's now estimated there are three times as many bureaucrats per student as there are lecturers and professors.

It's been a similar story in Britain. Here, too, the bureaucracy has been put on steroids. So much so that by the end of the 2010s, academic Sue Shepherd revealed there had been a 55% increase in the number of 'pro vice-chancellors' in the country's oldest universities, while other researchers have likewise tracked a sharp rise in the number of senior bureaucrats and an explosion in the amount of money our apparently cash-strapped universities are spending on bureaucracy.[3]

This was confirmed in 2021, when, remarkably, a major report from King's College London found that the number of senior managerial and administrative posts in UK universities had exploded by some 60% in just twelve years, rising from 32,000 administrative positions in 2006 to nearly 51,000 by 2018.[4]

While some of this reflects the swift expansion of higher education and the need for universities to do more things, such as looking after their rapidly growing numbers of international students and serving the new obsession with 'student satisfaction' on campus, the growth of this bureaucracy has also come with many problems, which professors like me have witnessed first-hand.

For a start, this vast and unwieldy bureaucracy is cutting the system of higher education adrift from the reality of academic life. Whereas in the past professors like me stepped up, albeit reluctantly, to help run the university, ensuring it was shaped by people who teach students, carry out research and respect the virtues of academic life, today things are very different.

Many of the administrators who now wield enormous power and influence have no real research or teaching experience and are appointed from outside the university, often after careers in finance and business, and so have little if any serious interest in teaching, research, academic freedom and, to be frank, education itself.

As fellow professor Benjamin Ginsberg points out in his book *The Fall of the Faculty*, rather than keep teaching, research and academic freedom at the heart of the university, today's bureaucrats often see these things merely through the lens of the university's corporate 'brand', and so will happily sacrifice them if and when they are thought to conflict with the public image of this brand. This is why senior administrators are often among the first to call for challenging speakers and controversial scholars to be silenced and shut down, lest they bring 'negative' or 'problematic' media attention to the university, or undermine the new obsession with student satisfaction.[5]

One example of this was researcher Noah Carl,

whom we first encountered in chapter 2, being thrown out of Cambridge. Why? Because the master of the college concerned, Matthew Bullock, a former banker who had spent his working life not in academia but finance, appeared to cave to the student mob, sacrificing academic freedom on the altar of appeasing that mob and wanting to minimize any negative publicity.

In this way, while the university bureaucracy becomes less experienced in academic matters the university environment also becomes sterilized, cleared of anything that might be problematic for the bureaucrats. The individual characteristics, ideas and passions of the teaching staff are replaced by a set of homogeneous, regulated and board-approved systems.

Routinely, too, many of these senior bureaucrats are rewarded for failure, with administrators who have led universities into the financial abyss simply moving on to bigger and better posts elsewhere in the sector. It is not uncommon, for example, for a senior bureaucrat who has presided over massive failure simply to emerge in another senior administrative post at another university, just as we have become used now to the news reporting on similar sideways shuffling in the corporate world.

In 2024, in Britain, astonishingly, despite universities being engulfed by a financial crisis, at least two-thirds of their already grossly overpaid vice-chancellors took pay rises; of sixty-six universities known to be making academics redundant and imposing cost-cutting measures, forty-three somehow found the money to give their vice-chancellor a rise, with many on deals worth over £400,000 a year.[6]

One striking example is Teesside University, which despite announcing a voluntary severance scheme for its academics still handed its vice-chancellor a 17% rise on their total salary package, which rocketed to more than £364,000 a year. This is considerably more than what the Prime Minister is paid. In fact, 170 vice-chancellors in Britain today earn more than the PM, despite presiding over big deficits and failing institutions.[7]

Even more shockingly, as recently as 2019 a study by the University and College Union found that 109 vice-chancellors in the 135 universities it approached for information attend the very meetings that decide their pay.[8] One example is Dame Glynis Breakwell, former vice-chancellor of Bath University, who was not only the highest paid university leader in the country, on £468,000 a year, but who enjoyed an interest-free car loan of £31,000 and a £20,000 fund for expenses – which she once used to claim £2 for biscuits. Like many other vice-chancellors, Breakwell sat on the very remuneration committee which hiked her pay, and which was filled with other senior bureaucrats who had no incentive to rock the boat. In this case, her salary rocketed by nearly £200,000 in only five years – while presiding over a university that kept many of its academic staff on precarious and unstable fixed-term and zero-hours contracts.[9]

Nor is Bath unique. While university leaders routinely proclaim that their institutions represent liberal progressive values such as fairness and equality, in 2023 the Higher Education Statistics Agency revealed that more than one in three academics in the UK – equivalent to about 80,000 people – were employed on such contracts.[10] Once again there is a palpable hypocrisy running through these institutions which, on the one hand, present themselves as communities that care deeply about their members but which, on the other hand, consistently fail to apply this ethos to their own staff, who are often left hanging in vulnerable positions.

As journalist Adrian Wooldridge points out: 'Life within many universities no longer resembles the bucolic ideal that those of us of a certain age remember. A tiny tenured elite sits on top of a mass of toiling temporary workers who move from one short-term assignment to the next, and frequently end up unemployed – the world's most highly educated lumpenproletariat.'[11]

The fact of the matter, notes Wooldridge, is that in recent decades, as their bureaucracy expanded, many universities have simply imported the worst qualities of mature companies, losing touch with their founding ideals. Exorbitant CEO pay. A bloated middle-management and bureaucracy. A tendency to treat non-tenured and hence less secure academics as dispensable workers. And, to the annoyance of conservatives who once argued that this 'marketization' of higher education would dilute academic radicals and raise standards, it has also opened the door to a corrosive identity politics which has lowered standards and brought 'the expensive paraphernalia of the woke corporation'.

I experienced this first-hand while watching a close friend and colleague try to navigate their academic career after finishing their PhD. Rather than the university giving my friend a permanent, full-time contract with security and employment rights, each year it would offer them another fixed-term contract for eleven months of the year. Why eleven months? Because if the contract extended to a full year and was renewed over several years then the university would have to make them a permanent member of staff, with those accompanying protections and entitlements. So, instead, the university just kept them dangling from one eleven-month contract to the next. Even worse, they made my friend a spokesperson for diversity and equality issues, asking them to speak at University Open Days about the wonders of various fairness initiatives.

In 2018, a Channel 4 *Dispatches* documentary drew attention to this glaring hypocrisy on campus by revealing that despite academics having their pensions slashed and their average annual pay rising by only 1%, and despite many of them being kept on fixed-term and zero-hours contracts, and despite tuition fees being raised and students being squeezed to the maximum at every possible turn, senior bureaucrats and vice-chancellors continued to enjoy five-star hotels, fine dining and first-class travel, paid for out of the university coffers. After submitting Freedom of Information requests to 157 universities, the documentary revealed that vice-chancellors and senior administrators had spent nearly £8 million in expenses over a two-year period, including on Michelin-star restaurants, one lunch with a £405 drinks bill, and a £1,300 work of art.[12]

These scandals are outrageous. But the proliferation of this bureaucracy and the growing power of this system is eroding university life in a far more profound way, as it undermines and compromises the neutrality of our institutions.

Increasingly, as bureaucrats have amassed more power and influence – setting the rules, priorities and procedures on campus – they have redefined the very ethos and purpose of universities, and not in a good way. In recent years, as we'll see, this bureaucracy has morphed into a kind of hyper-political and highly activist managerial blob that has moved to entrench the new ideology, politicizing the universities along the way.

This is symbolized, among other things, by the proliferation of political insignia on campus such as rainbow lanyards and flags (which are usually placed in the centre of campus as though marking a pseudo-religious shrine), the removal of supposedly 'racist' statues, the renaming of 'racist' buildings, the imposition on students of politically motivated reading lists, the use of political tests in applications for academic jobs and grants, and openly discriminating against political minorities in the name of non-discrimination.

At the very heart of this process – the politicization of the university – has been the relentless rise of the diversity, equality (or in America 'equity') and inclusion (DEI) agenda, an assortment of policies and procedures that are rapidly reshaping universities, public institutions and corporations around openly political goals.

Before setting out the problems with this, it's worth looking at the numbers involved to get a sense of the sheer scale of the agenda that in recent years has been sweeping through and upending university life.

In America, in 2024, the University of Michigan was revealed to be paying more than $30 million to some 241 DEI bureaucrats each year, enough to cover the tuition fees for nearly 2,000 students. Thirteen of these administrators are paid more than $200,000 a year, and it's the same story at other universities, like Virginia, which has spent $20 million annually on 235 DEI workers, some of whom were paid more than $580,000 a year.[13] At the University of California, Berkeley, the number of people working in its 'equity and inclusion' division rocketed from 110 in 2017 to 170 in 2022, with the university spending $25 million each year on DEI.[14]

Some readers might think this is unique to America, where DEI has had an especially tight grip over campus. But that would be wrong. In Britain, in 2023, a study by the non-partisan Alumni for Free Speech (AFFS) sent Freedom of Information requests to more than fifty universities, asking them how much they spend on the DEI agenda compared to protecting free speech. The results were just as striking.

While universities complain about spiralling costs and a financial crisis, the AFFS found that forty-two of the universities that responded to its requests were collectively spending more than £19.5 million annually on DEI staff and advice, at a cost of almost £500,000 per university per year – more than enough to cover a year's tuition fees for fifty undergraduate UK students at each university.[15] Overall, the universities that responded to AFFS hired more than 500 staff to work on DEI but only five to work on protecting free speech. Britain's elite universities, the study concluded, were spending 214 times more money on the DEI agenda than they were spending on protecting and promoting free speech.

One example is the prestigious St Andrews, Scotland's

oldest university. In 2023, it was revealed the university was spending nearly a quarter of a million pounds on equality and diversity staff while spending nothing at all on protecting freedom of speech – despite St Andrews being rated by think-tank Civitas as among the most restrictive of all when it comes to free speech. Furthermore, the university has also appointed to its court activists from radical political campaign groups such as pro-LGBT rights group Stonewall and the activist charity Advance HE (which we'll discuss later), which is incompatible with its supposed institutional neutrality.[16]

Other reports by conservative groups suggest that the amount of money universities in Britain are now spending on DEI initiatives could be even higher than we currently think. In 2022, a report by Conservative Way Forward suggested Britain's universities could be spending more than £30 million each year on more than 700 DEI roles, and are devoting 30,000 staff training days to 'equality training'.[17] The examples range from the University of Oxford (according to the report) employing forty members of staff at a cost of £2 million a year, to the University of Bristol employing seventeen people with combined salaries over £750,000.

Despite continually complaining about a financial crisis and putting dozens of its own academics at risk of redundancy, in 2024 Aston University advertised a £98,000-a-year post in 'People, Culture and Inclusion'.

Despite slimming down mathematics and music programmes as a cost-cutting drive, Oxford Brookes
managed to find money to appoint an 'anti-harassment'
and DEI adviser on £39,000 a year. And despite record-
ing a £25 million deficit and pushing academics to take
voluntary severance, Open University managed to fill
two DEI jobs, paying salary packages of nearly £50,000
a year, including a 'gender equality' officer who had to
attend campus 'at least twice a year'.[18]

The rapid growth and expansion of the DEI agenda
is problematic because of how, alongside the leftward
shift among academics which we charted in chapter 2,
it is further corrupting institutions that are supposed to
be neutral. While many readers will think 'What is the
problem with DEI?', at its core it is a political project,
implemented to pursue a political agenda.

As centre-left writer Yascha Mounk points out,
while the duties and views of the rising number of university administrators vary, it is immediately obvious to
anybody who steps on to campus that many of them are
now actively promoting the new obsession with identity politics which finds its expression through DEI.

Whether knowingly or not, through a proliferation
of policies and procedures which are then imposed
in top-down fashion on staff and students, university
administrators are often promoting highly contested,
unscientific and openly political concepts, ideas and
theories, many of which are drawn from radical gender

ideology, critical race theory (CRT), intersectionality, post-colonial theory, and more.

While many HR departments present these ideas and concepts – such as 'white privilege', 'systemic racism', 'unconscious bias', 'whiteness', 'toxic masculinity', and more – as though they are established fact, in reality they are highly disputed ideas that are drawn from radical theories and often lack sufficient evidence.

Yascha Mounk, for example, points to Offices of Student Affairs offering students seminars on 'Understanding White Privilege' and 'Stay Healthy, Stay Woke', administrators at the University of California telling students to avoid 'offensive' phrases such as 'melting pot', and universities empowering bureaucrats to intervene when students use 'microaggressions' in conversation with one another, even encouraging them to report one another on anonymous hotlines.[19]

In Britain, too, there are countless examples of how the university bureaucracy has adopted the same outlook, becoming openly political and biased in the running of the university, reshaping its internal structures and culture around these highly political and contested ideas.

In 2021, for example, Cambridge introduced a new initiative that planned to encourage students and scholars to inform anonymously on one another if they felt they might have suffered a 'microaggression', with guidance published online suggesting that one such microaggression involved a member of the university raising an eyebrow while somebody from a minority background was speaking. Classically when it comes to university administrators and the incentive structure that guides them, the university only backtracked when the 'Change the Culture' initiative attracted negative publicity, after which the website for aspiring informants was suddenly taken down.

Other examples, as Professor Doug Stokes points out, are endless. Edinburgh University administrators telling staff that anybody who questions the 'lived experience' of non-white students and staff – such as questioning whether they really are living in 'institutionally racist' societies – is guilty of a 'microaggression'. Administrators at Imperial College claiming that the Enlightenment belief that there is 'only one race, the human race' is also 'microaggressive racism', and that the claim the 'most qualified person should get the job' is 'a racial microaggression'.

Or administrators at St Andrews introducing compulsory modules on diversity that students *must* pass before they are allowed to progress. One such test asks them: 'Does equality mean treating everyone the same?' Those who say yes are told this is incorrect because 'equality may mean treating people differently, and in a way that is appropriate to their needs so that they have fair outcomes and equal opportunity'. This is a powerful example of how the new ideology tells students that discriminating against some groups in the name of anti-discrimination is allowed, so long as it supports 'diversity' and 'social justice'.

What these examples reflect is how an entire university administration is now being built up around the diversity, equality and inclusion agenda, creating a growing army of well-paid, comfortable and usually non-academic officials who are personally incentivized to spread this agenda because they owe their salaries, positions and power to it.

At the same time, a minority of activist scholars support these changes because they see them as an extension of their radical progressive beliefs. In 2024, think-tank More in Common found that while not even half of British people think 'work around diversity, equality and inclusion leads to fairer outcomes', this rockets to 80% among radical left progressives who, as we saw in chapter 1, dominate the universities and are routinely pushing them to entrench DEI work on campus.[20]

But what is the problem with DEI, you might continue to ask? Who could possibly have a problem with nice-sounding words such as 'diversity', 'equality' and 'inclusion'? The answer, as a growing number of writers are pointing out, is that this agenda is the very opposite of what it claims to be.

As we'll see, it is undermining genuine *diversity* by insisting that there is no acceptable alternative to the narrow set of values and priorities upheld by the new ideology and its accompanying theories of 'social justice', 'critical race theory' and 'intersectionality'. Far from encouraging diversity, this agenda is rapidly rewiring universities around the highly political and contested claim that majorities are oppressing minorities, people are only defined by their fixed group identities, Western nations are inherently racist and oppressive, and, in turn, discrimination against some identity groups can be justified in the name of anti-discrimination.

It's undermining genuine *inclusion* by encouraging universities to exclude and marginalize scholars, students and speakers who dare to challenge or oppose this new ideology on campus, variously imposing new speech restrictions and language codes to silence and shut down nonconformist voices. Even the most passive individuals who do not hold the 'right' beliefs, who do not have the 'right' politics and who are not from the 'right' groups are often excluded or intimidated.

And it's eroding genuine *equality* – the idea that every man or woman should be judged on the same basis as an individual, within a meritocracy – by demanding the opposite: that we should categorize individuals into competing identity groups and treat them differently on the basis of their identity. The words 'equality' or 'equity', in other words, are routinely used instead to justify the unequal treatment of people.

Along the way, the DEI agenda is transforming universities into highly political, biased and ideologically driven institutions which prioritize the pursuit of dogma over truth, and which tell staff and students there is only one valid perspective – that of the new belief system. Contrary to an earlier generation of scholars in the 1960s and 1970s who, as we will see in the final chapter, argued that while individual academics and students could certainly express their political views the university itself must not become an openly political vehicle, the rewiring of the university apparatus around DEI is doing exactly this, using the agenda to impose political criteria on scholars, students and other staff.

It's important that we unpack these points in turn. One useful starting point is Paul Brest and Emily Levine, two scholars at the elite Stanford University who in 2024 explained, in the *New York Times*, why the DEI agenda is problematic.[21]

They rightly point out that, while many well-meaning liberals who support this agenda are driven by good intentions, in reality they are instead embedding a worldview that is deeply problematic and incompatible with the core values of higher education. Many of the DEI programmes, training packages and materials that are used on campus, write Brest and Levine, are simply too ideological, too radical, too biased and too reductive. As a result, they exacerbate the problems they intend to solve while suggesting that there is no viable alternative.

One way they do this is by undermining the goal of turning our young people into well-rounded, balanced, critical thinkers. DEI programmes and training routinely and crudely divide students and staff into only one of two categories, with little if any nuance. Either people belong to the oppressor majority group (i.e. white, male, straight) or one of the oppressed racial, sexual or gender minorities.

In 2021, for example, two Jewish employees filed official complaints against Stanford University's Counselling and Psychological Services division after, they claimed, its DEI programme, seminars and committee engaged in racial segregation by separating people from different identity groups into 'race-based affinity groups'. This saw bureaucrats describe all Jews as 'white or white-passing and therefore complicit in anti-Black racism'. Staff were crudely divided into just two groups: those who belonged to a group for 'people of color' and those, including Jews, who were lumped into a 'white accountability group'. The complaints were settled on confidential terms.[22]

Around the same time, Michigan State University was revealed to have promoted 'affinity groups for conversation within identity groups', whereby a separate group for white students was designed to provide 'time and space to work explicitly and intentionally on understanding white culture and white privilege and to increase one's critical analysis around these concepts', and a separate group for 'people of color' was held to 'work with peers to address the impact of racism, to interrupt experiences of internalized racism, and to create a space for healing and working for individual and collective liberation'.[23]

Reflecting its underlying logic, the DEI agenda has also led many universities and colleges, especially in America, to promote 'affinity graduation celebrations', whereby university students are separated into identity groups along the lines of their racial, ethnic, cultural or sexual characteristics, and are even given cords representing their identity group which they wear during graduation, and separate certificates alongside their diplomas.

In 2024, for example, elite Harvard University proudly published a gallery of pictures from its separate affinity graduation celebrations for black graduates, graduates with disabilities, graduates from Asian American, Pacific Islander and Desi-American backgrounds, Jewish graduates, first-generation low-income students, Indigenous graduates, Latinx graduates, veteran graduates and Arab graduates.[24]

These graduations are the very opposite of what an earlier generation of civil rights campaigners wanted to see, on the basis that they highlight what differentiates racial, ethnic, gender and other groups rather than what brings them together as members of a shared community.[25]

Some universities in America have even introduced so-called 'identity-based housing', which is racial segregation in another name. In 2021, Western Washington University introduced a designated housing area specifically for black students to 'explore and celebrate the diversity of Black and African American people and culture . . . creating a safe environment for open, honest, and sometimes challenging dialogue'.[26] Similar schemes have been introduced at institutions such as Stanford, Pacific Lutheran University, Oregon State University and Cornell University. In 2020, in response to the conviction of police officer Derek Chauvin over the death of George Floyd, American University in Washington DC announced that it would offer 'Black Affinity Housing', separating black students from white students in the name of promoting 'social justice'.

Instead of correcting stereotypes about other groups and people, note Brest and Levine, this growing obsession with DEI programmes, training and identity-based initiatives has also been shown by studies to reinforce stereotypes about some groups while imposing an agenda which, to be blunt, does not have the positive effect it claims to have.

In 2024, for example, in Britain, a major report for the government by an independent panel found remarkably little evidence that diversity, equality and inclusion efforts in public sector institutions, such as mandatory 'anti-bias training', were having any positive impact on corporate culture. 'The terms "diversity", "inclusion" (and other associated terminology) are conceptually ambiguous, rapidly evolving, and often conflated,' the authors of the report wrote, while suggesting that while diversity along racial, sexual and gender lines is the current obsession, diversity in terms of viewpoints and perspectives might be more important in encouraging efficiency and prosperity.[27]

Studies that look at what happens when you teach people about heavily contested concepts such as 'white privilege' have also found that contrary to its aims this makes white elites less sympathetic towards low-income whites.[28] It is, in other words, a luxury belief – an ideology that makes white elites feel morally righteous and good about themselves while simultaneously reducing their empathy for disadvantaged whites who are the most likely to be struggling with economic problems and to be left behind.

DEI programmes, note Brest and Levine, also reinforce other problems on campus, such as encouraging students to embrace a victimhood mindset, pitting different groups against one another on the basis of their group identities, and breeding resentment, especially among students who are discriminated against simply because they happen to belong to the 'wrong' identity group.

In 2023, Cambridge planned to bar white working-class students from applying to one of its postgraduate courses on the grounds that it wanted places to be reserved for children from minority ethnic backgrounds – before bureaucrats were forced to reverse their position after concerns were raised.[29] In the same year, the taxpayer-funded University of Minnesota sought to exclude white pupils from applying for paid summer internships, which administrators wanted to restrict to 'persons of colour' or Native Americans.

At the same time, King's College London was revealed to have left white staff feeling excluded after offering free t'ai chi classes that were 'aimed at combating chronic stress experienced in the body as a result of racism and systemic oppression'. The event was advertised as being for 'staff who identify as black/people of colour/global majority', with the term 'global majority' now used to try and elevate minorities above white majorities in Western states.[30]

In 2024, a 'whistle-blower' at the University of Washington revealed that its psychology department openly discriminated against whites and Asians by giving a tenure-track assistant professorship to the third-placed job applicant, who was African American. White staff were also excluded from attending meetings with job candidates while staff openly discussed ways to get around a US Supreme Court ruling which barred this kind of affirmative action on campus.[31] I experienced this countless times when, ahead of advertising an academic job in our department, the internal conversation would usually focus on somebody saying something like 'Our department is too white, we need to hire somebody of colour', or 'We have too few female professors, we need to hire a woman'. Routinely, the suggestion was that these identity characteristics were more important in the initial stages of recruitment than a candidate's actual ability.

There are many other examples of this open discrimination. A few years earlier, in 2019, academics and student leaders in Britain took to media to criticize the suggestion that racism against white students should be taken just as seriously as racism against minority students, accusing the organizations that did this of 'drawing a false equivalence'. Apparently, racism and discrimination only matter when they are directed towards non-white students.[32]

This discrimination in the name of anti-discrimination has also been visible during the university admissions process where, in recent years, universities and colleges, especially in America, have openly discriminated against some identity groups, such as high-performing Asian American students, in the name of diversity, equity and inclusion. In America, despite the US Supreme Court outlawing the practice of affirmative action in 2023, making it illegal for universities and colleges to consider race in their admissions decisions, many universities and colleges have continued to factor in race, exploiting ambiguities in the ruling and encouraging students to mention or reveal their race.

In 2024, for example, the campaign group Students for Fair Admissions, which believes that racial preferences during the admissions process are unfair, unnecessary and unconstitutional, wrote to the Yale, Princeton and Duke universities expressing their grave concern that these elite schools were not complying with the ruling. Looking at the most recent admissions data, the group argued that it simply was not possible for these schools to obtain the racial outcomes for their class of 2028 without in some way taking students' race into account during the admissions process, thereby breaking the law.[33]

The Johns Hopkins University in Baltimore, Maryland, for example, asks prospective students to 'tell us about an aspect of your identity (e.g. race, gender, sexuality, religion, community, etc.) or a life experience that has shaped you as an individual', while Rice University in Texas asks students: 'What perspectives shaped by your background, experiences, upbringing, and/or racial identity inspire you to join our community of change agents at Rice?'[34] This obsession with race-based admissions over a genuine meritocracy, where the brightest students rise to the top irrespective of their race and ethnicity, has been directly encouraged by the DEI agenda.

This agenda, furthermore, is deeply problematic because of how it stifles free speech and academic freedom and, in turn, strengthens a dogmatic and oppressive groupthink. Like scholars who are conservative or gender-critical, those who question whether universities should be this strongly influenced by an openly political diversity agenda have often been shunned.

As a fellow professor, Kevin Wallston, pointed out in 2023, there are good reasons to ask whether the DEI agenda is compatible with institutions that are supposed to prioritize the pursuit of truth, free speech and free expression. DEI offices, he points out, such as the one at the University of California, Los Angeles, openly state that 'although freedom of expression and freedom of inquiry form bedrock principles central to our mission to pursue knowledge and understanding . . . freedom of speech is . . . limited by other rights and values, such as equality'. Furthermore, when Wallston looked at the relationship between the size of a university's DEI bureaucracy and support for free speech and academic freedom, he found that universities which had larger DEI bureaucracies were less tolerant of conservative speakers and more supportive of disrupting actions to prevent speech on campus. Larger DEI bureaucracies on campus, in other words, correlate with more illiberal attitudes towards free speech among students.[35]

In 2020, for example, as part of a drive that would have looked completely normal in the Soviet Union under the notorious KGB, Sheffield University hired twenty students to challenge offensive language on campus, and report staff and students to 'racial equality champions' if they were thought to have offended others. One of the microaggressions included asking 'Why are you searching for things to be offended about?' – which is, apparently, offensive. As journalist Tom Slater remarked at the time: 'Those of us who write about campus censorship are often told we're mad tabloid alarmists who see Stasi-like behaviour everywhere. But then universities advertise for students to march around campus monitoring potentially offensive conversations and intervening where they deem appropriate.'[36]

Much of this oppressive climate and the chilling of free speech is also promoted by the larger satellite organizations that surround universities. The Equality and Human Rights Commission (EHRC), for example, encourages universities to continually be on the lookout for 'microaggressions' on campus, which could include: a lecturer's body language, non-white students allegedly being given less work than their white peers, students taking the stairs instead of a lift that contains students from minority backgrounds, and the allegedly damaging effects of Brexit, which it claims introduced a 'cold wind' on campus.

Interestingly, however, while university bureaucrats police things like 'microaggressions' and 'whiteness' on campus, they say little about the plight of the Uyghurs and other minorities who are being pushed into 're-education' camps in China. In 2019, for example, Vice-Chancellor Stephen Toope announced that Cambridge would be examining its historic links to the slave trade – even a bell was removed from one college because it was suspected of being linked to slavery. Yet at the very same time, Toope devoted considerable effort to deepening Cambridge's ties with China, gaining more funding from them and allowing this funding to influence the direction of the university. In my twenty years of teaching and working in universities I never once saw similar efforts to encourage Chinese students to reflect on their own history, cultural practices or links with slavery and imperialism.

Another specific way the DEI agenda suffocates free speech, undermines the neutrality of universities and erodes the academic freedom of scholars is through the use of 'diversity statements', which professors like me are routinely required to submit when applying for prestigious research grants and academic jobs.

Diversity statements are one or two sheets of paper which the person who is applying for a job or research grant must submit to the selection panel, explaining how their teaching and research contribute not to the pursuit of truth and the acquisition of knowledge but to promoting DEI.

This was standard in my career. I simply could not apply for a grant or academic job without first outlining my commitment to DEI – essentially being forced to swear allegiance to political dogma. Like other academics who belong to the political minority on campus – whether because they hold conservative or gender-critical views, or simply oppose the politicization of the university – I just went along with it, because if I hadn't submitted these statements I would simply never have secured a grant or job. During one interview for a major research grant, I was even asked by somebody on the interview panel – an external reviewer who was not even an academic – to explain how my personal views promoted diversity, equality and inclusion. It was just another example of how the system continually moves to isolate people who challenge the orthodoxy, and ensure they can be removed from jobs and grants.

Given how universities have moved sharply to the left, it's unsurprising to find that diversity statements are popular among academics. Surveys across the West have found that professors in the social sciences support them by a margin of almost two to one.

But whatever your political views, the use of such statements is very clearly a political litmus test, designed to promote candidates who support the new ideology while weeding out those who do not. Somebody who writes something like 'I do not believe teaching and research should be reshaped around openly political goals', for example, would almost certainly never get the job or research grant, especially when most people on the interview panel lean strongly to the left and believe the opposite.

Another academic who points to the glaring problem with these statements and the DEI agenda more generally is physicist Lawrence Krauss, who, writing in the *Wall Street Journal*, explained how things have changed on campus during his long career.[37] While it was certainly true that many scientific disciplines had too few women and minorities in the 1970s and the 1980s, he noted, from the 1990s things began to swing too sharply in the other direction. 'As chairman of a physics department in the 1990s, I had to write a statement justifying each appointment we made that went to a white man.' Once entrenched, 'the DEI offices began to grow unchecked. They became huge and expensive offices not subject to faculty oversight and now work to impose "equity" not only by discriminating in favor of female and minority candidates but by demanding and enforcing ideological commitments from new faculty.'

This radically changed the hiring process. Whereas

traditionally applicants for academic jobs had to submit published research articles, recommendations from their mentors and colleagues, and a statement of their proposed research and teaching interests, all of which would be assessed by university selection committees, by the 2010s it was the DEI agenda rather than the scholarly achievements of applicants that was the decisive factor.

'Several years ago,' continued Krauss, 'one began to see an additional criterion in advertisements for faculty openings. As a recent Cornell ad puts it: "Also required is a statement of diversity, equity and inclusion describing the applicant's efforts and aspirations to promote equity, inclusion and diversity through teaching, research and service."' At the time Krauss was writing, in 2021, of the twenty-five most recent advertisements for junior jobs in his field, no fewer than twenty-four demanded that applicants demonstrate an explicit, active commitment to DEI. Meanwhile, departments such as Life Sciences at the University of California, Berkeley, astonishingly, rejected some 76% of all applicants based on their diversity statements without looking at their record on research.

His colleagues, Krauss went on, were also writing to him to complain about how their white male postdoctoral students were not getting interviews for lectureships or had simply chosen to leave universities altogether, no longer convinced they had a chance of getting a job because they were white men.

Another way in which the system imposes the new dominant ideology from above is through 'anti-racism' (or 'diversity') training in teaching and research. Increasingly, scholars, staff and universities are pushed not just to say they reject racism and discrimination but to embrace a highly aggressive, divisive and activist brand of 'anti-racism' drawn from critical race theory (CRT).

In sharp contrast to the calls for colour-blind anti-racism which were made by civil rights campaigners in the past, this more aggressive model of anti-racism essentially calls for discrimination against whites, Asians and men in the name of ensuring 'equal outcomes' for historically disadvantaged racial, sexual and gender minority groups. Just look at what its proponents say.

Today, it's not uncommon for the system of higher education and university bureaucrats to promote the likes of Ibram X. Kendi, whose book *How to Be an Antiracist* has gone mainstream on campuses across the West. Kendi contends, with remarkably little empirical evidence, that every act, person, institution and policy cannot be neutral – it is either racist or anti-racist. People who describe themselves as 'not racist' are, in his mind, aligning themselves with the slave traders, segregationists and racists of the past. To have moral value, to be considered socially acceptable, you must redefine yourself as an active 'anti-racist', working continuously to dismantle what critical race theorists argue are endemic systems of racism and oppression in the West.

In turn, writers like Kendi openly advocate discrimination and racism in the name of tackling discrimination and racism. As he writes: 'The only remedy to racist discrimination is antiracist discrimination. The only remedy to past discrimination is present discrimination. The only remedy to present discrimination is future discrimination.'[38] Robin DiAngelo, another prominent writer promoted on campus, makes similar arguments, claiming that, essentially, all white people are racist and if they deny they are racist then that too is evidence of racism. As Yascha Mounk points out, books by the likes of DiAngelo and Kendi popularized the new dominant ideology on campus, promoting a non-falsifiable theory – namely, that any disagreement with the new orthodoxy is tantamount to racism.

These ideas have become rife on campus, pushed on by radical activist scholars and administrators who ignore evidence to the contrary, like the fact that levels of racial prejudice in Britain have been declining, not rising, in every major academic survey that has been collecting data since the 1980s. As I summarised in my last book, *Values, Voice and Virtue*, among reliable measures of prejudice, support for interracial relationships has shown a sharp increase over the last forty years, while at the same time the share of people who reject the idea that you have to be 'white to be British' has soared, to nine in ten people.[39]

Yet this has not stopped activist academics demanding that universities be completely reshaped around these dubious and disputed theories. In 2022, for example, a group of academics in Britain wrote an article in the leading magazine for the sector, *Times Higher Education*, titled 'How to be an anti-racist ally on the university campus'. Their highly political advice for scholars and students included embracing a range of contested ideas and concepts as though they were established fact.

Today's universities and academic departments, they argued, should embrace 'allyship' (i.e. actively supporting the rights of a minority group without being a member of it, while also being an 'active anti-racist') by acknowledging that combating privilege requires concrete action; establish yet more working groups and leadership on DEI activities; embed this work in every university department and school; demand that every school and department delivers an action plan on how they will pursue DEI work; appoint DEI 'student champions' who are given serious influence over decision-making bodies; call out people who say they 'don't see racism' or they 'don't see colour' on campus;

remind staff and students that when dealing with racism 'silence is a privilege too' and so one must always speak out; and focus on 'decolonising curricula', including inviting colleagues to explore their own identity, privilege and intersections, and developing 'decolonising toolkits' with students who are similarly urged to become 'allies' and help their academic lecturers and professors 'check their assumptions'.[40]

Much of this is reinforced from the top down by the system that surrounds the universities, comprising an amorphous and unaccountable blob of charities, organizations, lobby groups and more. The British charity Advance HE, for example, runs a membership scheme for universities. Through its 'Equality Charters' and 'Race Equality Charter', Advance HE urges universities to apply for a bronze, silver or gold award to showcase their commitment to the equality and diversity agenda. This includes signing up to the core principles of its Race Equality Charter, which means publicly accepting that 'racism is an everyday facet of UK society', that 'racial inequalities may manifest themselves in everyday situations, processes, and behaviours', that 'racial inequalities are not necessarily overt, isolated incidents', and 'embracing intersectionality . . . can better support institutions to tackle racism within the higher education sector'. While few people would reject the suggestion that some racism lingers on in Western societies, these organizations are encouraging universities to sign up to a particular view of racism and group relationships that is enshrined in CRT, which contends that every disparity among different racial and ethnic groups is due to engrained racism and discrimination among white majority populations and that institutions within their societies are inherently biased and discriminatory towards minority groups.

University applications to these schemes, furthermore, are reviewed by other academics, bureaucrats and 'equality and diversity practitioners'. The aim, as the charity states on its website, is 'to drive forward the cultural and systemic changes needed if institutions are to remain competitive and attractive to talented staff and potential students in a global market'.[41]

In 2021, Advance HE even published a document called *Tackling Racism on Campus Assets*. It was drafted by a working group of DEI managers from several prominent universities. Once again, the document uncritically advocated the very controversial and contested 'anti-racism' ideas within CRT, criticizing staff and students who showed 'white indifference' (which is itself said to be one step away from 'white supremacy'). According to the report, such people can be easily identified because they are 'passionate defenders of western universalism, academic freedom, and the right to offend'.[42] On campus, 'anti-racism training' or 'diversity training' is then used to immerse and indoctrinate staff and students in these academic theories, with students and staff often having to complete this mandatory training if they are to progress on to the next year of study or the next step on the academic career ladder.

The problem, however, is that this training has been shown to be based on dubious if not completely flawed methods. Researchers at Harvard and Tel Aviv University studied thirty years of diversity training data from more than 800 US companies and concluded that mandatory diversity training programmes had no effect on employee attitudes – and sometimes activated bias and racial hostility. As one recent comprehensive review of anti-racism or diversity training in the *Annual Review of Psychology* concluded, after struggling to find it having any positive effects, 'We suggest that the enthusiasm for, and monetary investment in, diversity training has outpaced the available evidence that such programs are effective in achieving their goals.'[43]

Another example of how the system is actively politicizing the university is by mainstreaming the 'decolonization' agenda, once an obscure idea from 'post-colonial' theory that is now being imposed wholesale on many universities.

Post-colonial theory is a highly activism-oriented area of study, in which academics advocate the systematic undoing of colonialism in all its forms, view societies as defined by power imbalances between the oppressed and oppressor groups, and aim to completely rewrite history, culture and knowledge from the perspective of 'oppressed' or 'colonized' minorities, even if this conflicts with objective knowledge and empirical evidence. They wish to 'decolonize' things in order to reduce a reliance on white scholars and writers from former 'colonizing' powers, promote voices from minority backgrounds and formerly colonized regions, irrespective of the quality of their research and work, and also criticize, problematize and disparage knowledge that is 'Western'.[44]

Much of this, too, is infused with the highly political and contested claim that all Western universities (and societies) are institutionally racist, and, in turn, their reading and teaching should be reshaped, essentially, around an explicitly anti-Western agenda, not least through decolonizing reading lists for students.

In 2020, amid the George Floyd and Black Lives Matter protests, the British think-tank the Higher Education Policy Institute published a report calling for 'the decolonisation of universities', which it argued 'is vital for the improvement of course curricula, pedagogical practice, staff wellbeing, and the student experience'.[45] Two years later, in 2022, a research report by Civitas suggested that 70% of universities in the UK were now undertaking some form of decolonization, either through official policies or individual academics advocating for it.[46]

The problem with reshaping the university around the decolonization agenda is that this approach routinely flies in the face of what should be at the centre of the university experience – objective knowledge, neutrality, reliable methodology, empirical evidence. Influenced by postmodernism, it argues that objective knowledge is infused with cultural values, and because much knowledge in the West was shaped by white and Western values then this is an injustice that must be remedied, while true rigour and understanding come not from evidence, scientific method and the like but, instead, the 'lived experience' and identity-based standpoints of minority, colonized groups.

Much of this agenda, furthermore (as Professor Doug Stokes points out in his book *Against Decolonisation*), not only ignores a considerable amount of empirical evidence which shows how universities are *not* systematically racist – such as the fact, as I have mentioned, that students from minority backgrounds routinely outperform their white counterparts – it also, curiously, ignores a great degree of colonialism, imperialism, racism and slavery that has taken place in non-Western states, such as the Ottoman Empire's development of the white slave trade of the Barbary states, or the black slave plantations in West Africa.[47] 'One could go on,' writes Stokes, 'but the point is that the decolonising of the curriculum movement is in danger of reproducing a simplistic account of human history of western villains and non-western heroes that once again places Europe as centre-stage.'

The imposition of the decolonization agenda, he notes, is further stoking a creeping illiberalism and technocratic managerialism on campus. And much of it is being pushed on by the wider system of higher education, which is using its growing power and influence to impose these ideas from the top down.

In Britain, for example, the Quality Assurance Agency (QAA) is an independent body which provides 'quality assurance' for teaching, with universities paying to be members and to receive its recommendations. In 2022, remarkably, the QAA revised its guidance to include a much stronger focus on what it called 'wider social goals', which included a specific emphasis on DEI. It advised academics to include these highly contested political concepts and ideas in their teaching, embedding them in the university. Professors in Classics were told to highlight 'imperialism, colonialism, white supremacy, and class division'. In Geography, they were told to draw attention to 'a variety of progressive theoretical perspectives', including 'but not limited to, theoretical perspectives from critical theory, critical race theory, decoloniality, disability studies, feminist, queer, and science and technological perspectives'. In History, they were told to engage closely with work to 'decolonise the curriculum, including challenging Eurocentric conceptual frameworks'.

As the Committee for Academic Freedom noted, while individual academics should be free to discuss these issues if they wish, this should ultimately be a decision for individual scholars; it should not be for a centralized body such as the QAA to advise that all courses include concepts, beliefs and topics that are subject to substantial academic debate, presenting them as though they are established fact.[48] Such guidance, the committee warned, reinforces a culture of orthodoxy and groupthink on campus while making a mockery of the organization's claim to be neutral. This is why Oxford University withdrew from QAA, with its former chancellor, Lord Patten, describing its guidance as 'the most dangerous assault in the last few years on freedom of expression and research at universities'.[49]

In 2020, similarly, the advocacy organization Universities UK, which claims to be 'the collective voice of 141 universities' and works with the government and higher education sector to 'champion UK higher education', published a report titled *Tackling Racial Harassment in Higher Education*.[50] It argued that including books on reading lists by white scholars perpetuates existing inequalities and is unlikely to reflect the experiences of many students and staff. In turn, it called on students to monitor and audit their courses to ensure 'the representation of diversity within materials used in lectures and tutorials', while instructing universities to ensure staff are trained to 'incorporate the concepts of white privilege and white fragility, white allyship, microaggressions and intersectionality, as well as racialised unconscious bias training'.

Through building an 'inclusive culture and environment by setting the tone and expectations of student and staff behaviour', senior managers will inaugurate a truly 'anti-racist' university. If this is resisted, those same managers are asked to 'commit' to there being 'consequences' when the drive for inclusivity is in any way 'breached'. As Stokes rightly points out, when political pressure is applied to scholars by organizations such as Universities UK, vice-chancellors and senior bureaucrats to adopt the ideology of decolonizing the curriculum as the correct and only way to approach research and teaching, a line has been crossed.

Much of this, once again, is deeply hypocritical. While the system of higher education urges universities and academics to decolonize their reading lists and campuses, reshaping them around an anti-Western agenda, they simultaneously adjust their reading lists and course content to please Chinese students and Chinese Communist Party (CCP) censors from a lucrative overseas market. 'Universities,' notes Professor Doug Stokes, 'are thus both decolonising the curriculum for the sins of yesterday's aristocrats while recolonising the curriculum for the sons and daughters of today's CCP.'[51]

These efforts to decolonize the university, as Professor Eric Kaufmann points out, reflect a core feature of the new ideology, which he describes as its 'deculturating thrust'. This worldview aims not only to challenge but to criticize and undermine the culture and historical legacy of Western nations so as to bring shame and guilt on majority groups within these nations. Attacking national heroes, tearing down statues and recasting national stories and history as tales of racist shame and prejudice, notes Kaufmann – such as efforts to remove statues of individuals linked to the slave trade at Goldsmiths, University of London; the removal of a dolphin emblem of slave trader Edward Colston by Bristol University; Cambridge's effort to remove a plaque commemorating a slave trade investor; Oxford's All Souls College's decision to drop Barbados-born slave owner Christopher Codrington's name from its library; and ongoing efforts to remove monuments to Cecil Rhodes at Oxford – do not simply reflect an attempt to 'make room for other voices'. For Kaufmann, they instead represent an attempt to undercut the pride of white majorities in Western nations and level them down so as to promote minorities who, conversely, *are* allowed if not encouraged to celebrate and defend their distinctive history, identity and culture.

As American activist and writer Christopher Rufo points out, the blunt reality is that many of the DEI programmes that are operating on campuses today should not be operating. 'These are not neutral programs to increase demographic diversity,' he wrote in the *New York Times* in 2023, 'they are political programs that use taxpayer resources to advance a specific partisan orthodoxy.'[52] And he has a point.

Over the last few decades, the rapid expansion of the university bureaucracy, the sharp shift to the left among university academics and the politicization of the wider system of higher education have left universities in a perilous state. Together, these changes are compromising the neutrality of these once great institutions, eroding free speech and academic freedom, and betraying their original purpose.

Routinely, today, universities are pushing professors like me to accept dubious and highly contested claims and theories about race, sex, gender, history and Western nations as though they are established fact when, in reality, they often have no serious basis in science or objective knowledge because they are neither verifiable nor falsifiable. Yet still we are told to 'decolonize' our reading lists, spend time engaging in flawed 'diversity' or 'anti-racism' training, submit political statements when applying for jobs or research grants, and generally work in a wider culture and climate in which the university is being openly politicized. Too many universities, once bastions of the pursuit of truth through the accumulation of scientific knowledge, reason, good faith debate and empirical research, have continued to peddle such things. And so, along the way, they have been further transformed from neutral institutions that once delivered a world-leading education to institutions that are now openly biased, highly political and delivering a bad education.

Which raises the obvious question: what might we do to address and fix these problems before it is too late?

5

Solutions

In 2024, I packed up my belongings in my office, threw my books into some boxes, and left campus for the last time. My professorship – everything I had ever wanted, everything I had ever worked for – was over.

I'd devoted twenty years of my life to climbing the academic ladder – to teaching countless students, marking essays and exams, publishing books and papers, giving research presentations at conferences around the world, and sitting in endless committees, intent on making a meaningful impact on the lives of young people. And now I was walking away.

As I said at the start of this book, pretty much everybody in my life thought I had gone insane. Who walks away from a secure job with good pay, a great pension, lots of autonomy, and the chance to travel the world?

The answer is somebody who has simply had enough of all the things I've pointed to in this book. While I made the decision to leave in 2024, as a financial crisis engulfed my university, my decision had been a much longer time coming, shaped by all the individual events, moments, scandals, mobbings and attempted cancellations I'd witnessed on campus over the years. From one scandal to the next, from one friend being harassed or sacked to the next, from one example of shocking political bias to the next, I could simply no longer walk on to campus each day trying to convince myself that I was working in a neutral institution that remained committed to the pursuit of noble goals.

Because, as I hope has become apparent, this is not the case. Instead, like a growing number of academics in the West, I reluctantly concluded that I was working in deeply biased, openly political, highly activist and ideologically homogeneous institutions that had morphed into havens for 'liberal' intolerance, a crushing groupthink and bureaucratic overreach. Institutions that are damaging and denigrating the scholars who violate this groupthink, are betraying the students and their families who are relying on them for a good education, and using the wider system of higher education to impose a political agenda, from the top down, on everybody else.

I became tired of watching a radical activist minority of self-described 'liberals' and 'progressives', supported by a growing army of hapless bureaucrats, discriminate against my friends and colleagues simply because they happened to hold different views from them. I became tired of watching truth, evidence and free speech being sacrificed on the altar of pseudo-religious dogma. I became tired of watching a widespread assault on viewpoint diversity, forcing countless people to hunker down and self-censor.

Along the way, I also became steadily more disillusioned with watching our once great universities appear increasingly willing to betray the very things they're supposed to prioritize – truth, free speech, academic freedom – in the name of dubious and highly contested political goals and theories such as 'social justice', 'critical race theory' and 'diversity, equality and inclusion'.

Could I have stayed and stuck it out for another twenty years? Sure. Just look around. Universities are filled with resentful, disillusioned and depressed academics who either don't have the courage to leave or don't know what else to do with their lives. But what kind of life is that?

So, as I walked off campus for the last time, I felt a profound sense of relief. By walking away from my professorship, by choosing to do something else with my life, I no longer had to play a role in delivering an education I didn't believe in.

Now, as I said at the start of the book, many of the people who are still working and teaching in the universities will simply deny my account. They'll say none of this is true, that it's misleading, or has been wildly exaggerated.

This is why I wanted to include as much evidence

as I could, much of it from large, reliable and robust surveys, reports and studies. I've bombarded you at times with statistics and research because I wanted you to read it for yourself and make up your own mind. Hopefully I've convinced you that rather than these problems being unique to me, to the story of just one professor at just one university, they are in fact a microcosm of much wider trends that are now sweeping through and undermining universities.

And I think this deeply worrying evidence tells us a remarkably clear and consistent story: we have a very big problem. Which raises an obvious question. If we want to keep these institutions at the very heart of our societies, if we want to stop other people from leaving, and if we want to restore public confidence and trust in them, then how exactly might we fix them?

This question is especially important given how many of the problems I've pointed to in this book are now spilling out into other institutions in society.

From government departments to mainstream media, from big tech to the creative industries, from publishing to cultural institutions, many of the people reading this book will recognize the things I experienced in their own work. The creeping intolerance, the oppressive climate, the restrictive speech codes and censorship, the political activism disguised as 'diversity, equality and inclusion', the self-censoring, and the bullying, harassment and isolation of people who happen to hold unfashionable views.

As British writer Andrew Sullivan once said, the reality, whether we like it or not, is that we all live on campus now. 'When elite universities shift their entire worldview away from liberal education as we have long known it toward the imperatives of an identity-based "social justice" movement,' he has written, 'the broader culture is in danger of drifting away from liberal democracy as well. If elites believe that the core truth of our society is a system of interlocking and oppressive power structures based around immutable characteristics like race or sex or sexual orientation, then sooner rather than later, this will be reflected in our culture at large.'[1] What matters on campus, in other words, is now what matters across the West.

This is because while universities have certainly lost their way, they remain important and influential institutions. By publishing research, by teaching the next generation of citizens, influencers and leaders, and by shaping the parameters of truth, science and evidence – or what philosopher Jonathan Rauch has called 'the constitution of knowledge' – universities still set the tone for many other institutions in society, our culture and politics.[2] So, we really do need to try and fix them before it's too late.

And I think there are essentially two ways we might

do that. There's what we might call the classically liberal or 'defensive' approach, and then there's what we might call the interventionist or 'assertive' approach.

The classically liberal approach suggests that we should try and fix universities by engaging with the wider culture in an effort to steer it in a less restrictive direction and hope that these institutions, and the people who lead them, respond positively. We should 'have a conversation', 'trigger a debate', have a 'meaningful discussion' about the challenges I've outlined in this book.

We should, in other words, spend the next few years trying to convince the radical progressives, leftists and politically motivated bureaucrats who now dominate the universities that crucial things like free speech and academic freedom are worth protecting and promoting and that, together, we all need to push back against the growing threats to them on campus.

Many prominent liberals have made exactly this argument. A few years ago, in 2020, a large group of famous intellectuals and writers – Margaret Atwood, Steven Pinker, J. K. Rowling, Malcolm Gladwell, among many others – joined together to write a spirited open letter in *Harper's Magazine*. They warned, much like I've warned in this book, against a 'new set of moral attitudes and political commitments that tend to weaken our norms of open debate and toleration of differences in favor of ideological conformity'.[3]

The forces of illiberalism, they pointed out, are gaining strength across the West, reflected in a new intolerance of opposing views, a vogue for public shaming and ostracizing others, restricting debate, and seeking to punish those who are seen to violate politically correct speech and thought.

What was their proposed remedy? 'The way to defeat bad ideas is by exposure, argument, and persuasion, not by trying to silence or wish them away.' In short, they advocated that we take on the new illiberalism by doubling down on liberalism itself, by putting our faith in the free speech, free expression and good faith debate that lie at the heart of the liberal project.

This is an admirable argument. It is also why, in recent years, several organizations, think-tanks and foundations have emerged to try and nudge universities into doing exactly this, applying pressure from the outside in the hope that they will listen and respond by changing their policies and procedures.

One example is Heterodox Academy, a membership organization for scholars, staff and students 'who want to ensure that our universities are places where intellectual curiosity thrives', and which works 'to advance open inquiry, viewpoint diversity, and constructive disagreement across higher education'. How does it do this? By holding conferences and workshops, conducting surveys of scholars and students to highlight threats to free speech and academic freedom – some of which

I've used in this book – and raising public awareness about these wider challenges on social media.

Or the Foundation for Individual Rights and Expression (FIRE), which aside from also running public education campaigns and surveys tries essentially to shame universities into reforming themselves by publicly ranking them according to their commitment to free speech and expression.

These are important organizations doing important work. And, as I say, the underlying argument that we can defeat illiberalism by doubling down on liberalism itself is admirable and seductive.

But I think it is also deeply naive and misguided.

Why? Well, for a start, I don't think this defensive strategy comes close to meeting the sheer scale of the challenge I've outlined in this book, which is rooted in an aggressive ideology that is continually looking for ways to expand, spread its tentacles, and dominate the way these conversations are held.

This ideology is stronger and more deeply entrenched than many of its critics think. As many leading experts have tracked in detail – Eric Kaufmann, Yascha Mounk, Chris Rufo and Francis Fukuyama among them – the ideas and theories that are driving this ideology forward are at least forty years old, if not older. They've also continued to spread despite similar calls for discussion in the past. From earlier debates about political correctness in the 1980s and 1990s to today's about cancel culture, the new ideology has only become stronger, not weaker, over time. I don't see how yet another spirited discussion about free speech will make a difference.

As we saw in previous chapters, furthermore, when you look at the attitudes and beliefs of the younger scholars and students who are making their way through the universities and higher education system there are also good reasons to expect this challenge only to strengthen in the years ahead. Today's young Zoomer students from Generation-Z and their Millennial lecturers, as the evidence we explored makes clear, are much more likely than their older counterparts to support the silencing of dissenting views, the imposition of censorship and the harassment of political minorities, and to want to prioritize political goals at the expense of free speech and academic freedom.

It will take a lot more than a few 'debates' or 'reasserting liberal values' by ageing Baby Boomers, in other words, to overcome the tide of progressive illiberalism that's sweeping through the universities and which will, the evidence suggests, only grow in strength in the years and decades to come.

Furthermore, unlike in the past, the rapid expansion of the university bureaucracy and the diversity, equality and inclusion (DEI) agenda has created an entirely new layer of incentives for academics, bureaucrats and university leaders to entrench the new ideology on campus, reshaping universities around its openly political, divisive and unscientific priorities.

The reason why the discrimination against political minorities, the use of political litmus tests when hiring scholars or distributing research grants, politically motivated reading lists, and training if not indoctrinating staff and students in political propaganda have all become more visible on campus is because there are, today, very real motives for doing these things. If you are a university bureaucrat, you have good reason to promote the ongoing politicization of the university because your job depends on it; if you are a radical activist scholar you have good reason to promote it because you strongly believe in it; and if you are a moderate scholar who is just trying to keep your head down then you too are likely to go along with it, or at least unlikely to challenge it, because you want to protect your career, and certainly don't want to fall foul of the radical mob and be ostracized or, worse, cancelled.

Unlike in the 1980s, 1990s and 2000s, in other words, there are now real, powerful and tangible incentives for academics and administrators to continue to promote or at least tolerate the new illiberalism on campus, which reflects how the universities and much of the surrounding system have been corrupted.

And this is why a growing number of people – myself included – are arguing that the classically liberal or defensive approach to the crisis on campus is simply insufficient to deal with the scale of this challenge.

While interventionists such as Eric Kaufmann, Christopher Rufo and others might not have written about the crisis on campus from a personal perspective, as I have done in this book, in their writing they do converge on the same point: namely, that if we really want to save universities in the West then we are going to need a stronger response that is capable of tackling the new illiberalism head-on.

Interventionists, for a start, begin with the view that allowing an alliance of radical activists and bureaucrats to continue to run roughshod over the traditional virtues of academic life while well-meaning liberals 'have a debate' and hope this will trigger much-needed changes on campus is unacceptable. Taxpayer-funded, public institutions that are responsible for developing our young people, interventionists point out, should not have the right to censor if not harass and exclude students and staff, politicize higher education, and impose a narrow set of highly contested political beliefs on everybody else.

And if we are supposed to believe that universities and higher education really will reform themselves, they ask, then why have they consistently failed to do so for much of the last fifty years? Why have universities allowed their faculties and departments to shift so strongly to the left? Why, when scholars have been bullied, ostracized and sometimes sacked, have more universities not spoken out against this intolerance? And why did many senior scholars and administrators remain ominously silent during the most egregious cases, including some that we have explored in this book, from Kathleen Stock and Noah Carl in Britain to the likes of Roland Fryer in America?

The answer to these questions, say interventionists, is that universities cannot be trusted to reform themselves. Even when proposed reforms have been introduced, from the pushback to DEI in America to a new law to protect free speech and academic freedom in Britain, universities have spent considerable time and resources opposing, not supporting, these moves.

This is why, as we saw in chapters 1 and 2, self-censorship and the like have become and remain rife on campus. Many staff and students can see how their university's disciplinary procedures, bureaucracy and culture have not changed at all and remain strongly opposed to any serious change.

And this is why, unlike the classically liberal approach, interventionists argue that the only way to fix universities is to use government to enshrine in law the protection and promotion of free speech and academic freedom.

Seen from this perspective, only government action and new legislation, or pressure from outside universities, can change the incentive structures on campus. This means adopting a proactive rather than a passive strategy, making it clear that the individual freedom of scholars and students is, ultimately, more important than the freedom or autonomy of the university.

Many academics and administrators will recoil from this suggestion, not only because it threatens their dominance over the universities but because, in their eyes, any intervention in university life will be seen as 'authoritarian'. They will complain of government overreach.

But, as Professor Eric Kaufmann points out, there are many examples from history where intervention in such matters was not just preferable but required. Think, for example, even just in the last decade, of police departments riddled with sexism and corruption, religious communities captured by radical preachers, school networks covering up rampant paedophilia, medical organizations plagued by misconduct, political parties rife with antisemitism, or tech giants abusing their power. In these cases and more, when institutions have become deeply corrupted or ideologically lopsided, we do not simply step back and allow them to continue undermining the rights and freedoms of individuals. We do not wait and hope they will reprimand themselves and change course.

On the contrary, we intervene, using the powers of the state to restore justice and balance – and we should now intervene in the universities and higher education, to push back against authoritarianism, political corruption and ideological bias, and ensure that the freedom of scholars and students, even if they are a minority, is protected and promoted.

What might this interventionism look like? One approach would be to force universities, through government action, to sign up to the so-called 'Chicago principles' – a set of guidelines intended to demonstrate a commitment to freedom of speech and freedom of expression on campus.

Initially adopted by the University of Chicago in 2014, the Chicago principles (or 'Chicago Statement') articulate the university's commitment to free, robust and uninhibited debate and deliberation among university staff. The principles, since adopted by more than a hundred universities in America, commit the university to free and open enquiry in all matters so long as it does not break the law, warn that concerns about civility and mutual respect must never be used to justify the closing down of debate, 'however offensive or disagreeable those ideas may be to some', and guarantee that all members of the university community have the broadest possible latitude to speak, write, listen, challenge and learn.

Furthermore, the Chicago principles are explicit in stating that 'it is not the proper role of the University to attempt to shield individuals from ideas and opinions they find unwelcome, disagreeable, or even deeply offensive'.

Requiring universities to sign up to this code of best practice and embedding it firmly within the wider culture of higher education would be a good start. So too would requiring them to commit to the Kalven Committee report, which was also published by the University of Chicago, in 1967, and outlines the desired role of the university when it comes to political and social action.

Crucially, it insists on maintaining the university's neutrality on political and social issues. The university, noted the committee, will always be 'the home and sponsor of critics', namely individual scholars and students who should be free to criticize the government and world around them. But the university itself, as an institution, must not morph into a critic. It must 'maintain an independence from political fashions, passions, and pressures'.

Perhaps sensing the future direction of universities in the West, it stressed the fact that universities are not clubs, trade associations or lobbies. They do not exist to take collective action on the big issues of the day. Nor should they insist that their staff and students adopt a particular view on a social policy or social movement because to do so would inevitably mean censoring a minority of staff and students who might not agree.

'The neutrality of the university as an institution,'

concluded the Kalven Committee, during the heady days of the 1960s, 'arises then not from a lack of courage nor out of indifference and insensitivity. It arises out of respect for free inquiry and the obligation to cherish a diversity of viewpoints.'

While individual scholars and staff should always have the freedom to engage in political action and social protest as individuals, the university itself must remain neutral and not be diverted from its core mission into 'playing the role of a second-rate political force or influence'.

And to this, lastly, we can add the recommendations of the Shils report, also published by Chicago, in the early 1970s, which focused on how universities should appoint their scholars and staff.

Instead of universities conducting political litmus tests, as they are doing today through means such as 'diversity statements' and politically imbalanced selection panels, the Shils report recommended that the political beliefs and affiliations of academic job candidates should have no influence on the decision to hire them. The only criterion that should guide the hiring process, argued the group of academics who were instructed to reflect on these issues, is academic merit – namely, the candidate's research excellence, teaching experience, and their commitment to serving the university and the wider community. Their personal beliefs, opinions and values should not influence the outcome.

What this means, in practice, is removing things like diversity statements from the recruitment and research grant process, no longer asking candidates for their views on political criteria like the DEI agenda, and ensuring that recruitment panels give as much weight to the political diversity of their members as racial, sexual and gender diversity – if not, ideally, removing such things from the recruitment process altogether.

How practical are these ideas, and how could they be implemented in the real world? Well, when it comes to universities in Britain, I did not leave my job without a fight. Between 2018 and 2024, I was one of only a handful of professors, lecturers, policymakers and lawyers who genuinely tried to reform the universities and ensure they protected and promoted free speech. Disillusioned and depressed about many of the things I've discussed in this book, we formed a secretive, underground network of rebels who tried to push back against the creeping tide of intolerance on campus.

Specifically, we helped design and develop the Higher Education (Free Speech) Act, which eventually passed through Parliament and received Royal Assent in 2023. The law created a legal requirement for universities and higher education providers to protect and promote free speech and academic freedom on campus within the limits of existing law, not just publish admirably phrased but ultimately meaningless statements that make little difference on campus.

Crucially, it also created a new body, an Academic Freedom Directorate, that could penalize universities should they fail to do these things. It established the role of a 'free speech tsar', who would have the power to fine universities and allow scholars and students who had reasonably exhausted the existing complaints system to sue universities that violated their freedoms.

Had this free speech law existed when many of the contrarian scholars we have met in this book were intimidated, harassed and sacked then the universities that presided over these shocking cases would have faced serious consequences.

Those scholars and students who felt that their right to free speech, free expression and academic freedom were being hampered could now turn to an external organization, outside the university, for support and action which, in turn, would help to encourage wider cultural change on campus. The last thing universities want is to be dragged through lengthy procedures, fined and publicly shamed for violating things like free speech. Knowing universities are required to do these things would also, arguably, help restore public trust and confidence in these institutions which, as we've seen, is currently collapsing.

Revealingly, even before the law was passed the mere

knowledge of this intervention and government action had started to produce a visible culture shift on campus. Universities like Cambridge implemented new free speech codes while I and other academics were invited to institutions like Oxford to take part in a new series of 'free speech debates' for undergraduate students, ensuring they were exposed to a diverse range of opinions, beliefs and perspectives.

Some academics will therefore point out that we already have existing laws and legal protections for academic freedom and free speech, which is true; but the long list of violations of these freedoms on campus, many of which have been discussed in this book, reflect how these laws are only rarely enforced and often appear toothless to many. Furthermore, as I pointed out, the informal and indirect pressures at work in universities are often suffocating these rights and freedoms below the radar, away from the public eye.

Moreover, while the law was passed by the 2019–24 Conservative government, in late 2024 the country's new Labour Prime Minister Keir Starmer and his Education Secretary, Bridget Phillipson, halted the introduction of the legislation, making it clear they wanted to repeal the Higher Education (Free Speech) Act altogether.

At the time of going to print, a group of academics and free speech campaigners who oppose Labour's move have applied for a judicial review of the decision, including the Free Speech Union, which says that Labour's decision to try and 'kill off' the law would make it 'virtually impossible for students and academics to challenge radical progressive ideology on campus'.[4]

Interestingly, reflecting one of the themes of this book, it was claimed that Labour's Education Secretary sought to shelve the free speech law at least in part 'because British universities wanted to protect their operations in authoritarian states such as China'. After being forced to respond to legal challenges from the Free Speech Union, government lawyers noted that 'concerns' had been raised with them about the 'consequences for delivering English [higher education] in foreign countries which have restrictions on free speech' (and which now also happen to be a major source of revenue from international students).[5]

While a source within the Department for Education played this point down, they claimed that the proposed free speech law 'could expose students to harm'. This is yet another example of what we've seen throughout this book, namely how appeals to protect the 'emotional harm' of students or minorities are now routinely prioritized over the defence of core liberties such as free speech and expression.[6]

But those of us who still care about what happens on campus should not be discouraged. Across America, for example, a growing number of colleges, universities and academic departments are rapidly rowing back on the DEI agenda, while calls to ban diversity statements and oppose cancel culture are growing by the day. At the time this book went to press (late 2024), the *Chronicle of Higher Education* tracked changes to DEI policies on 196 college campuses across twenty-nine states, with many states now simply banning DEI offices, diversity programmes and identity-based preferences.[7]

At the same time, there has emerged an increasingly active and well-funded ecosystem of alternative higher education providers, including the University of Austin, Ralston College and the Centre for Heterodox Social Science at the University of Buckingham, where in late 2024 I was delighted to accept a position as Senior Visiting Professor, having given up on the hope that the established universities will reform themselves.

In the first instance, the Centre for Heterodox Social Science will start to address the glaring political bias and lack of choice for young and mature students by offering the first ever course on woke ideology in the UK, ensuring that as much energy and effort is devoted to understanding the radical left as the established universities devote to understanding the radical right. Over time, with support and students, this will grow into a major research hub for scholars from across the political spectrum, where students will be genuinely exposed to a diverse range of theories, reading, opinions and beliefs, rather than a narrow, stifling groupthink.

Lastly, to my mind, because of the Chicago Principles,

the Kalven Committee report, the Schils report, the free speech law in the UK and the growing global pushback against illiberalism on campus, I do think it's now possible to draw up and share a manifesto of sorts that should guide future action, designed to repair, renew or simply save universities and higher education before it's too late – a manifesto, on the next page, that I will leave you, the reader, to ponder.

Manifesto

A university that is committed to good, not bad, education will commit to the following:

- Free and open enquiry in all matters, so long as it does not break the law, defame an individual or constitute a genuine threat or harassment.
- Guaranteeing all members of the university community the broadest possible latitude to speak, write, listen, challenge and learn.
- Respecting and supporting the freedom of all staff to discuss any problems openly and without negative consequences.
- Opposing the shielding of individuals from theories, ideas and opinions they find unwelcome, disagreeable, harmful or offensive.
- Opposing attempts to shut down debate and discussion through appeals to civility, mutual respect, or in the name of avoiding 'emotional harm'.
- Removing all internal speech codes and university policies that conflict with the above commitment to free speech and academic freedom.
- Requiring that all universities be regularly audited for academic freedom and free speech violations, with the ability to fine institutions that fail to

observe these basic protections for students and scholars.

- Requiring that universities devote as much effort to promoting political diversity on campus as they devote to promoting racial, sexual and gender diversity. Where DEI is promoted, if it is promoted at all, political diversity must be promoted to the same degree.
- Requiring universities to take political discrimination as seriously as they take racial, sexual and gender discrimination.
- Ensuring that individual academics retain complete control and autonomy over their course reading lists and are not subject to top-down university regulations that interfere with their academic freedom.
- Banning any direct relationship between political parties and universities, including funding, scholarships and placements for scholars and students.
- Banning the use of 'diversity statements' during the hiring of academics and the allocation of research grants.
- Ensuring that all research grant selection panels and search committees for academic and senior administrative jobs are politically balanced.

- Instead of all academic job applicants reflecting on how their research and teaching supports DEI, requiring them instead to reflect on how their research and teaching supports free speech, free expression and academic freedom on campus.

NOTES

CHAPTER I: WHAT HAPPENED TO YOU?

1 Though the idea of the university can be traced back much further, to Plato's Academy in Ancient Greece, the Library of Alexandria in Egypt, imperial academies in China, Buddhist monasteries in India, the libraries of Timbuktu, and ancient institutions in Baghdad and Morocco.

2 N. Ferguson, 'America's woke universities need to be replaced', *Bloomberg*, Nov 2021; available online: https://www.bloomberg.com/opinion/articles/2021-11-08/niall-ferguson-america-s-woke-universities-need-to-be-replaced

3 C. O. Callaghan, 'The world's top 100 universities', Top Universities, Nov 2024; available online: https://www.topuniversities.com/student-info/choosing-university/worlds-top-100-universities

4 A. Sullivan, 'What happened to you?', *The Weekly Dish*, July 2021; available online: https://andrewsullivan.substack.com/p/what-happened-to-you

5 B. J. M. Jones, 'U.S. confidence in higher education now closely divided', Gallup, July 2024; available online: https://news.gallup.com/poll/646880/confidence-higher-education-closely-divided.aspx

6 D. Belkin, 'Americans are losing faith in college education, WSJ-NORC poll finds', *Wall Street Journal*, Mar 2023; available online: https://www.wsj.com/articles/americans-

are-losing-faith-in-college-education-wsj-norc-poll-finds-
3a836ce1

7   YouGov, 'Are degrees from English universities good value
    for money', 2024; available online: https://yougov.co.uk/topics/
    society/trackers/are-degrees-from-english-universities-good-
    value-for-money; on too many young people going to
    university, see https://yougov.co.uk/topics/society/trackers/
    do-enough-children-go-to-university

8   Ferguson, 'America's woke universities need to be
    replaced'

9   H. Shearing, 'University student complaints hit record
    high in England and Wales for fourth successive year',
    BBC News, April 2023; available online: https://www.bbc.
    com/news/education-65324664

10 J. Chavda, 'Fewer young men are in college, especially at
    4-year schools', Pew Research Center, April 2024; available
    online: https://www.pewresearch.org/short-reads/2023/12/
    18/fewer-young-men-are-in-college-especially-at-4-year-
    schools

11 Student Academic Experience Survey 2024, Advance
    HE, June 2024; available online: https://www.advance-he.
    ac.uk/knowledge-hub/student-academic-experience-
    survey-2024

12 P. Foster, A. Gross and A. Borrett, 'The looming financial
    crisis at UK universities', *Financial Times*, Jul 2023; available
    online: https://www.ft.com/content/0aca64a4-5ddc-43f8-
    9bba-fc5d5aa9311d

13 D. Goodhart, 'Why universities had to be challenged',
    UnHerd, July 2020; available online: https://unherd.
    com/2020/07/why-universities-had-to-be-challenged

14   X. Xu, 'Increasing concentration of high-skilled jobs in
     London means graduates elsewhere cannot fully capitalise
     on their education', Institute for Fiscal Studies, Nov 2023;
     available online: https://ifs.org.uk/news/increasing-
     concentration-high-skilled-jobs-london-means-graduates-
     elsewhere-cannot-fully

15   T. Whelton, 'The State of the graduate premium',
     Intergenerational Foundation, Jan 2025; available online:
     https://www.if.org.uk/2024/01/17/the-state-of-the-graduate-
     premium

16   W. Tanner, J. O'Shaughnessy, 'The politics of belonging',
     UK Onward, 2019; available online: https://www.
     ukonward.com/wp-content/uploads/2019/10/Politics-of-
     Belonging-FINAL.pdf

17   M. Goodwin and R. Eatwell, *National Populism: The Revolt
     Against Liberal Democracy* (Penguin, 2018).

18   M. Sandel, *The Tyranny of Merit* (Farrar, Straus & Giroux,
     2020); see also Robert Putnam, *Our Kids: The American
     Dream in Crisis* (Simon & Schuster, 2015).

19   F. Fukuyama, *Liberalism and its Discontents* (Profile
     Books, 2022); Y. Mounk, *The Identity Trap: A story of
     ideas and power in our time* (Penguin, 2023); J. Haidt and
     G. Lukianoff, *The Coddling of the American Mind: How
     good intentions and bad ideas are setting up a generation
     for failure* (Penguin, 2018); Ferguson, 'America's woke
     universities need to be replaced'; J. McWhorter, *Woke
     Racism: How a new religion has betrayed Black America*
     (Penguin, 2021); E. Kaufmann, *Taboo: How making
     race sacred produced a cultural revolution* (Forum, 2024);
     K. Stock, 'How universities killed the academic', *UnHerd*,

Mar 2024, available online: https://unherd.com/2024/03/
how-universities-killed-the-academic; H. Pluckrose and
J. A. Lindsay, *Cynical Theories: How activist scholarship
made everything about race, gender, and identity – and why
this harms everybody* (Pitchstone Publishing, 2020); N.
Biggar, 'What's at stake in the culture wars?', *The Critic*,
Nov 2023, available online: https://thecritic.co.uk/whats-
at-stake-in-the-culture-wars; G. Lukianoff and R. Schlott,
*The Canceling of the American Mind: Cancel culture undermines
trust and threatens us all – but there is a solution* (Simon &
Schuster, 2023); A. Doyle, *The New Puritans: How the religion
of social justice captured the western world* (Constable, 2022);
C. Rufo, *America's Cultural Revolution: How the radical left
conquered everything* (HarperCollins, 2023).

20 Kaufmann, *Taboo*; see also Kaufmann, *Whiteshift:
Populism, immigration and the future of white majorities*
(Penguin, 2018).

21 Mounk, *The Identity Trap*.

22 Ferguson, 'America's woke universities need to be
replaced'.

23 Fukuyama, *Liberalism and its Discontents*.

24 D. Ben-David, '40 per cent of Russell group students
say October 7 attack was "resistance"', *Jewish Chronicle*,
May 2024; available online: https://www.thejc.com/news/
40-per-cent-of-russell-group-students-say-october-7-
attack-was-resistance-11q3r154

25 J. Haidt, 'Why antisemitism sprouted so quickly on
campus', *After Babel*, Dec 2023; available online: https://
www.afterbabel.com/p/antisemitism-on-campus

26 Kaufmann, *Taboo*.

CHAPTER 2: SCHOLARS

1   J. Morgan, 'EU referendum: nine out of 10 university staff back Remain', *Times Higher Education*, Jun 2016; available online: https://www.timeshighereducation.com/news/european-union-referendum-nine-out-of-ten-university-staff-back-remain

2   T. Hayward, 'The Banned List', Academics for Academic Freedom, Nov 2024; available online: https://www.afaf.org.uk/the-banned-list

3   Campus Deplatforming Database, 'The foundation for individual rights and expression', *FIRE Disinvitation*, 2022; available online: https://www.thefire.org/research-learn/campus-deplatforming-database

4   J. Bindel, 'Kathleen Stock: I won't be silenced', *UnHerd*, Nov 2024; available online: https://unherd.com/2021/11/kathleen-stock-i-wont-be-silenced

5   J. Benda, *Treason of the Intellectuals* (Eris, 2021; originally published 1927).

6   N. Ferguson, 'The treason of the intellectuals', *The Free Press*, Dec 2023; available online: https://www.thefp.com/p/niall-ferguson-treason-intellectuals-third-reich

7   J. Prinsley, 'University where students openly celebrated October 7 accused of "breeding terror"', *Jewish Chronicle*, Mar 2024; available online: https://www.thejc.com/news/uk/university-where-students-openly-celebrate-october-7-accused-of-breeding-terror-n9kk6b8v

8   A. Lapin, 'US university professors retract blaming Israel for Hamas massacre after censure', *Times of Israel*, Oct 2023; available online: https://www.timesofisrael.com/us-university-professors-retract-blaming-israel-for-hamas-massacre-after-censure

9 For a summary of this evidence in the United States, see
E. Kaufmann, 'Academic freedom in crisis: punishment,
political discrimination, and self-censorship', Center for
the Study of Partisanship and Ideology, Mar 2021; available
online: https://www.cspicenter.com/p/academic-freedom-
in-crisis-punishment

10 C. Flaherty, 'Voter registration data show Democrats
outnumber Republicans among social scientists, 11.5
to 1', Inside Higher Ed, Oct 2016; available online:
https://www.insidehighered.com/news/2016/10/03/
voter-registration-data-show-democrats-outnumber-
republicans-among-social-scientists

11 M. Langbert, 'Homogenous: The political affiliations of
elite liberal arts college faculty', National Association of
Scholars, Apr 2018; available online: https://www.nas.
org/academic-questions/31/2/homogenous_the_political_
affiliations_of_elite_liberal_arts_college_faculty

12 M. Langbert, 'Homogenous'.

13 C. Hanretty, 'Is the left over-represented within academia?',
Medium, Mar 2017; available online: https://medium.
com/@chrishanretty/is-the-left-over-represented-within-
academia-90b1cbe00e8a

14 Kaufmann, *Taboo*.

15 P. Norris, 'Cancel culture: Myth or reality?', Political
Studies (2021); available online: https://journals.sagepub.
com/doi/10.1177/00323217211037023

16 Matthew Goodwin, *Is Academic Freedom Under Threat?*
(Legatum Institute, 2022).

17 L. Conway, *Liberal Bullies: Inside the mind of the
authoritarian left* (Swift Press, 2024).

18 YouGov, 'Do Brits think that immigration has been too high or low in the last 10 years?', 2024, available online: https://yougov.co.uk/topics/politics/trackers/do-brits-think-that-immigration-has-been-too-high-or-low-in-the-last-10-years; YouGov, 'Would you support or oppose a move to increase the number of deportations of illegal immigrants from the UK?', Aug 2024, available online: https://yougov.co.uk/topics/politics/survey-results/daily/2024/08/21/9ef2c/1

19 C. C. Martin, 'How ideology has hindered sociological insight', *American Sociologist* (2015), cited by Noah Carl in an Adam Smith Institute paper ('Lackademia: Why do academics lean left', available online: https://static1.squarespace.com/static/56eddde762cd9413e151ac92/t/58b5a7cd03596ec6631d8b8a/1488299985267/Left+Wing+Bias+Paper.pdf).

20 'Scientific fraud and politics', *Wall Street Journal*, June 2015; available online: https://www.wsj.com/articles/scientific-fraud-and-politics-1433544688

21 R. Fryer, 'Roland Fryer tells the truth on race and policing', *The Free Press*, Feb 2024; available online: https://www.youtube.com/watch?v=IQ9tTottjB8

22 Jonathan Rauch, 'The Constitution of Knowledge', *National Affairs*, Winter 2022; available online: https://nationalaffairs.com/publications/detail/the-constitution-of-knowledge

23 H. D. Clarke, M. J. Goodwin and P. Whiteley, *Brexit* (Cambridge University Press, 2017).

24 OpenDemocracy UK, 'Framing ethnic diversity as a "threat" will normalise far-right hate, say academics', Oct 2018; available online: https://www.opendemocracy.net/

en/opendemocracyuk/framing-ethnic-diversity-debate-as-about-threat-legitimises-hat-0

25 R. Henderson, 'How the luxury beliefs of an educated elite erode society', *The Times*, Feb 2024; available online: https://www.thetimes.com/uk/article/how-the-luxury-beliefs-of-an-educated-elite-erode-society-0mx8fd2nl

26 T. Edsall, 'America has become both more and less dangerous since Black Lives Matter', *New York Times*, May 2023; available online: https://www.nytimes.com/2023/05/17/opinion/black-lives-matter-depolicing-homicides.html

27 E. Cooley, J. Brown-Iannuzzi, R. F. Lei and W. Cipolli III, 'Complex intersections of race and class: among social liberals, learning about white privilege reduces sympathy, increases blame, and decreases external attributions for white people struggling with poverty', *Journal of Experimental Psychology General*, 148 (12), 2218–2228, Dec 2019; available online: https://pubmed.ncbi.nlm.nih.gov/31033321

28 Academic Freedom Index, 2024; available online: https://academic-freedom-index.net

29 Kaufmann, 'Academic freedom in crisis'.

30 C. Flaherty, 'FIRE launches new database for tracking attacks on speech', *Inside Higher Ed*, Aug 2021; available online: https://www.insidehighered.com/news/2021/08/31/fire-launches-new-database-tracking-attacks-speech

31 Scholars Under Fire, 'Attempts to sanction scholars from 2000 to 2022', Apr 2023; available online: https://www.thefire.org/research-learn/scholars-under-fire-attempts-sanction-scholars-2000-2022

32 Scholars Under Fire, '2024 college free speech rankings',
    Sep 2023; available online: https://www.thefire.org/
    research-learn/2024-college-free-speech-ranking

33 R. Adekoya, E. Kaufmann and T. Simpson, *Academic
    Freedom in the UK: Protecting Viewpoint Diversity* (Policy
    Exchange, 2020).

34 Kaufmann, 'Academic freedom in crisis'.

35 N. Carl, 'Who Doesn't Want to Hear the Other Side's
    View?'; available online: https://noahcarl.medium.
    com/who-doesnt-want-to-hear-the-other-side-s-view-
    9a7cdf3ad702

36 Carl, 'Who Doesn't Want to Hear the Other Side's View?'.

37 YouGov survey 2019; available online: https://d25d2506sfb9
    4s.cloudfront.net/cumulus_uploads/document/1muyphj1
    6u/TheTimes_190114_BrexitFriendsandFamily_w.pdf

38 R. Roache, 'If you're a Conservative, I'm not your friend',
    Practical Ethics, May 2015; available online: https://blog.
    practicalethics.ox.ac.uk/2015/05/if-youre-a-conservative-
    im-not-your-friend

39 L. Woodhouse, 'What happened to the left?', *Substack*,
    May 2023; available online: https://public.news/p/what-
    happened-to-the-left

40 F. Attenborough, 'British universities have a China problem',
    The Critic, March 2024; available online: https://thecritic.co.
    uk/british-universities-have-a-china-problem

41 R. Kerbaj and S. Griffiths, 'Security services fear the march
    on universities of Beijing's spies', *Sunday Times*, Oct 2019;
    available online: https://www.thetimes.com/uk/article/
    security-services-fear-the-march-on-universities-of-beijings-
    spies-gv9pk3hzr

42 H. Joyce, 'Ditching this free speech act is a green light to campus bullies', *The Times*, August 2024; available online: https://www.thetimes.com/comment/columnists/article/ditching-this-free-speech-act-is-a-green-light-to-campus-bullies-v2wtjjptd

43 T. Karran and L. Mallinson, *Academic Freedom in the UK: Legal and Normative Protection in a Comparative Context* (UCU, 2017).

44 Kaufmann, 'Academic freedom in crisis'.

45 Matthew Goodwin, *Is Academic Freedom Under Threat?* (Legatum Institute, 2022).

46 R. S. Butcher, 'Universities: Is free speech under threat?', *BBC News*, Oct 2023; available online: https://www.bbc.co.uk/news/education-45447938

47 Joyce, 'Ditching this free speech act is a green light to campus bullies'.

CHAPTER 3: STUDENTS

1 D. Goodhart, *The Road to Somewhere: The populist revolt and the future of politics* (Oxford University Press, 2017).

2 G. Lukianoff and J. Haidt, 'The Coddling of the American Mind', *The Atlantic*, September 2015 issue; available online: https://www.theatlantic.com/magazine/archive/2015/09/the-coddling-of-the-american-mind/399356

3 B. Campbell and J. Manning, *The Rise of Victimhood Culture: Microaggressions, safe spaces, and the New Culture Wars* (Palgrave Macmillan, 2018).

4 Campbell and Manning, *The Rise of Victimhood Culture*, p.74.

5   Scholars Under Fire, 'Attempts to sanction scholars from 2000 to 2022', Apr 2023; available online: https://www.thefire.org/research-learn/scholars-under-fire-attempts-sanction-scholars-2000-2022

6   Jessica Blake, 'Teaching on Eggshells: Students report professors' offensive comments', *Inside Higher Ed*, 21 July 2023; available online: https://www.insidehighered.com/news/students/free-speech/2023/07/21/students-likely-report-instructors-offensive-comments

7   Civitas, *The Radical Progressive University Guide* (2023); available online: https://www.civitas.org.uk/content/files/Radical-Progressive-University-Guide-FINAL.pdf

8   M. Penn, D. Nesho, S. Ansolabehere, 'Harvard caps Harris poll', *The Harris Poll*, Oct 2023; available online: https://harvardharrispoll.com/wp-content/uploads/2023/10/HHP_Oct23_KeyResults.pdf

9   YouGov, 'Which side in the Israeli-Palestinian conflict do you sympathize with more?', Oct 2023, available online: https://yougov.co.uk/topics/politics/survey-results/daily/2023/10/16/b8bd3/1; YouGov, 'From everything you've seen and heard, do you think that Hamas are or are not a terrorist organisation?', Oct 2023, available online: https://yougov.co.uk/topics/politics/survey-results/daily/2023/10/13/be487/3

10 E. Kaufmann, 'The Politics of the Culture Wars in Contemporary Britain', Policy Exchange, 2022; available online: https://policyexchange.org.uk/wp-content/uploads/2022/11/The-Politics-of-the-Culture-Wars-in-Contemporary-Britain.pdf

11 'The Forgotten: How White Working-Class Pupils Have Been Let Down', Education Committee; available online:

https://committees.parliament.uk/committee/203/education-committee/news/156024/forgotten-white-workingclass-pupils-let-down-by-decades-of-neglect-mps-say

12 Gov UK, 'Widening participation in higher education, Academic year 2022/23', *Explore Education Statistics*, Oct 2024; available online: https://explore-education-statistics.service.gov.uk/find-statistics/widening-participation-in-higher-education

13 S. Coughlan, 'Half of universities have fewer than 5% poor white students', *BBC News*, Feb 2019; available online: https://www.bbc.co.uk/news/education-47227157

14 Higher Education Policy Institute, 'You Can't Say That! What Students Really Think of Free Speech on Campus', 2022; available online: https://www.hepi.ac.uk/wp-content/uploads/2022/06/You-cant-say-that-What-students-really-think-of-free-speech-on-campus.pdf

15 HEPI, 'You Can't Say That!'.

16 B. Duffy, 'The State of Free Speech in UK Universities: What Students and the Public Think', 2022; available online: https://www.kcl.ac.uk/policy-institute/assets/the-state-of-free-speech-in-uk-universities.pdf

17 E. Kaufmann, 'Academic freedom in crisis: punishment, political discrimination, and self-censorship', Center for the Study of Partisanship and Ideology, Mar 2021; available online: https://www.cspicenter.com/p/academic-freedom-in-crisis-punishment

18 'Why young men and women are drifting apart', *The Economist*, 13 March 2024; 'Changing fortunes drive young women's votes left and men's right', *The Times*, 2 April 2024.

19 Kaufmann, *Taboo*, p.260.

20 C. Clark and B. Winegard, 'Sex and the Academy. The Inclusion of Women in Higher Education is a Great Achievement for Western Liberal Societies. How is this Changing Academic Culture?', *Quillette*, 2022; available online: https://quillette.com/2022/10/08/sex-and-the-academy/

21 Clark and Winegard, 'Sex and the Academy'.

22 Heterodox Academy 2023 Campus Expression Survey (2024); available online: https://heterodoxacademy.org/campus-expression-survey

23 J. Bitzan and C. Routledge, '2021 American College Student Freedom, Progress and Flourishing Survey', Sheila and Robert Challey Institute for Global Innovation and Growth, 2021; available online: https://www.ndsu.edu/fileadmin/challeyinstitute/Research_Briefs/2021_American_College_Student_Survey.pdf

24 B. Duffy, 'The state of free speech in UK universities: what students and the public think', Kings College London, Sept 2022; available online: https://www.kcl.ac.uk/policy-institute/assets/the-state-of-free-speech-in-uk-universities.pdf

25 N. Ferguson, 'America's woke universities need to be replaced', *Bloomberg*, Nov 2021; available online: https://www.bloomberg.com/opinion/articles/2021-11-08/niall-ferguson-america-s-woke-universities-need-to-be-replaced

26 Duffy, 'The state of free speech in UK universities'.

27 Office for Students, Transcript of Arif Ahmed's speech at King's College London, July 2024; available online: https://www.officeforstudents.org.uk/news-blog-and-events/press-and-media/transcript-of-arif-ahmeds-speech-at-kings-college-london

28 H. Cass, 'The Cass Review', April 2014, p.13; available
online: https://cass.independent-review.
uk/home/
publications/final-report

29 'Cambridge don in trans row after boycotting gender-
critical speaker', *Daily Telegraph*, 21 October 2022; available
online: https://www.telegraph.co.uk/news/2022/10/21/
cambridge-don-trans-row-boycotting-gender-critical-
speaker

30 N. Carl, 'Cognitive ability and socio-political beliefs and
attitudes', PhD thesis, University of Oxford, 2017; available
online: https://ora.ox.ac.uk/objects/uuid:856fc58a-120f-
4a51-a569-422e201e9f61/files/mb95789685e6ae1a86fb4b
66dd069d095

31 N. Woolcock and G. Willoughby, 'Quarter of pupils with
three Ds at A-level get first-class degrees', *The Times*,
Sept 2024; available online: https://www.thetimes.com/uk/
education/article/university-degree-first-class-explained-
cmmg6ro3v

32 H. Lambert, 'The Great University Con: How the British
degree lost its value', *New Statesman*, August 2022;
available online: https://www.newstatesman.com/politics/
2019/08/the-great-university-con-how-the-british-degree-
lost-its-value

33 M. Jones Jr, 'I was fired from NYU after students
complained that the class was too hard. Who's next?', *Boston
Globe*, 20 October 2022; available online: https://www.
bostonglobe.com/2022/10/20/opinion/i-was-fired-nyu-after-
students-complained-that-class-was-too-hard-whos-next

34 'Growing disconnect between students and UK universities',
Times Higher Education, 4 March 2024; available online:

https://www.timeshighereducation.com/news/growing-disconnect-between-students-and-uk-universities

CHAPTER 4: SYSTEM

1   D. Stokes, 'The campus grievance industry', *The Critic*, Sept 2020; available online: https://thecritic.co.uk/issues/september-2020/the-campus-grievance-industry

2   P. Weinstein Jr, 'Administrative bloat at U.S. colleges is skyrocketing', *Forbes*, Aug 2023; available online: https://www.forbes.com/sites/paulweinstein/2023/08/28/administrative-bloat-at-us-colleges-is-skyrocketing

3   S. Shepherd, 'There's a gulf between academics and university management – and it's growing', *Guardian*, Jul 2017, available online: https://www.theguardian.com/higher-education-network/2017/jul/27/theres-a-gulf-between-academics-and-university-management-and-its-growing; see also J. Morgan, 'Market forces blamed for 30% increase in managers', *Times Higher Education*, 7 October 2010; and J. Hogan, 'Is higher education spending more on administration and, if so, why?', *Perspectives: Policy and Practice in Higher Education* 15 (1), 2011, pp.7–13.

4   King's College London, 'Report reveals big changes to staffing patterns at UK universities', Nov 2023; available online: https://www.kcl.ac.uk/news/report-reveals-big-changes-to-staffing-patterns-at-uk-universities

5   B. Ginsberg, *The Fall of the Faculty* (Oxford University Press, 2011).

6   E. Harding, 'Outrage as two thirds of vice chancellors at cash cutting universities are revealed to have taken', *Mail Online*, Aug 2024; available online: https://www.dailymail.

co.uk/news/article-13753513/Outrage-two-thirds-vice-chancellors-cash-cutting-universities

7 E. Busby, 'Repeated calls for pay restraint among university leaders "could be dangerous"', *Independent*, Aug 2023; available online: https://www.independent.co.uk/news/uk/university-and-college-union-higher-education-policy-institute-hepi-higher-education-statistics-agency-university-of-oxford-b2402242.html

8 University and College Union, '81% of vice-chancellors still allowed to attend meeting that sets their pay', UCU, June 2019; available online: https://www.ucu.org.uk/article/10163/81-of-vice-chancellors-still-allowed-to-attend-meeting-that-sets-their-pay

9 R. Adams, 'Bath University vice-chancellor quits after outcry over £468k pay', *Guardian*, Nov 2017; available online: https://www.theguardian.com/education/2017/nov/28/bath-university-vice-chancellor-quits-after-outcry-over-468k-pay

10 University and College Union, 'Precarious work in higher education', UCU, Aug 2023; available online: https://www.ucu.org.uk/media/14007/precarious-work-in-higher-education--update-August-2023/pdf/UCU

11 A. Wooldridge, 'Higher education in the US faces a systematic crisis', *Bloomberg*, April 2023; available online: https://www.bloomberg.com/opinion/articles/2023-04-18/higher-education-in-the-us-faces-a-systemic-crisis

12 J. Doward and L. Drevet, 'Flowers, drinks and a dog: vice-chancellors claimed £8m in expenses over two years, *Guardian*, Feb 2018; available online: https://www.theguardian.com/education/2018/feb/24/flowers-drinks-and-a-dog-vice-chancellors-claimed-8m-in-expenses-over-two-years

13 J. Kabbany, 'UMich now has more than 500 jobs dedicated to DEI, payroll costs exceed $30 million', *The College Fix*, Jan 2024, available online: https://www.thecollegefix. com/umich-now-has-more-than-500-jobs-dedicated-to-dei-payroll-costs-exceed-30-million; M. Horzempa, 'The Dollars and Cents of DEI', The James G. Martin Center for Academic Renewal, Mar 2024, available online: https://www.jamesgmartin.center/2024/03/ the-dollars-and-cents-of-dei

14 K. Wallsten, 'Is DEI causing the "Crisis of free speech" on campus?', Heterodox Academy, Dec 2023; available online: https://heterodoxacademy.org/blog/is-dei-causing-the-crisis-of-free-speech-on-campus

15 Alumni for Free Speech, 'Leading universities spend 214 times more on diversity staff than on free speech protection staff, according to our Freedom of Information data', *EDI and Free Speech at Universities*, Dec 2023; available online: https://affs.uk/edi-free-speech-universities

16 M. Smith, 'St Andrews University criticised for spending on diversity staff', *Sunday Times*, Apr 2023; available online: https://www.thetimes.com/uk/education/article/st-andrews-university-criticised-for-spending-on-diversity-staff-xwd3 ldvkd

17 Conservative Post, 'Professor hits out after report reveals universities are spending millions on diversity and equality training', Dec 2022; available online: https://conservativepost. co.uk/professor-hits-out-after-report-reveals-universities-are-spending-millions-on-diversity-and-equality-training

18 J. Henry, 'Universities axe hundreds of lecturers - then appoint "woke" diversity chiefs on £100k salaries', *Mail Online*, Apr 2024; available online: https://www.dailymail.co.

uk/news/article-13357949/amp/Universities-axe-hundreds-
lecturers-appoint-woke-diversity-chiefs-100k-salaries-
despite-nearly-half-UK-vice-chancellors-expect-university-
financial-deficit

19 Y. Mounk, *The Identity Trap: A story of ideas and power in
    our time* (Penguin, 2023), pp.100–102.

20 M. Stears, T. Soutphommasane, L. Tryl and A. Rajah,
    'Finding a balance – how to ensure equality, diversity and
    inclusion is for everyone', UCL Policy Lab, Mar 2024;
    available online: https://www.moreincommon.org.uk/our-
    work/research/finding-a-balance

21 P. Brest and E. Levine, 'D.E.I. Is Not Working on College
    Campuses. We Need a New Approach', Aug 2024;
    available online: https://archive.ph/nvRaH#selection-935.
    0-939.292

22 E. Redden, 'EEOC complaint against Stanford alleges
    DEI program created hostile environment for Jewish
    staff', *Inside Higher Ed*, June 2021; available online:
    https://www.insidehighered.com/news/2021/06/16/
    eeoc-complaint-against-stanford-alleges-dei-program-
    created-hostile-environment

23 M. Perry, 'Michigan State University gets caught illegally
    segregating "affinity groups" by skin color, then conceals
    it, and then backtracks', AEI, April 2021; available online:
    https://www.aei.org/carpe-diem/michigan-state-university-
    gets-caught-illegally-segregating-affinity-groups-by-skin-
    color-then-conceals-it-and-then-backtracks

24 J. Choe, 'Affinity celebrations for the class of 2024',
    The Harvard Crimson, May 2024; available online:
    https://www.thecrimson.com/article/2024/5/23/
    affinity-celebrations-2024-photo-essay

25 J. Alonso, 'Conservatives take aim at affinity graduation celebrations', *Inside Higher Ed*, May 2023; available online: https://www.insidehighered.com/news/students/diversity/2023/05/02/conservatives-rail-against-segregated-graduations

26 B. Zeisloft, 'Yet another school introduces race-based housing', *Campus Reform*, Sept 2021; available online: https://www.campusreform.org/article/yet-another-school-introduces-race-based-housing/18209

27 E. Hub, 'Inclusion at work panel: report on improving workplace diversity and inclusion', Gov UK, Mar 2024; available online: https://www.gov.uk/government/publications/inclusion-at-work-panel-report-on-improving-workplace-diversity-and-inclusion

28 E. Cooley, J. Brown-Iannuzzi, R. F. Lei and W. Cipolli III, 'Complex intersections of race and class: among social liberals, learning about white privilege reduces sympathy, increases blame, and decreases external attributions for white people struggling with poverty', *Journal of Experimental Psychology General*, 148 (12), 2218–2228, Dec 2019; available online: https://pubmed.ncbi.nlm.nih.gov/31033321

29 E. Somerville, 'Cambridge planned to block white students from applying for course', *Telegraph*, Feb 2023; available online: https://www.telegraph.co.uk/news/2023/02/25/cambridge-blocked-white-students-applying-one-postgraduate-courses

30 E. Somerville, 'Race row after white lecturers barred from university's "separatist" tai chi classes', *Telegraph*, July 2024; available online: https://www.telegraph.co.uk/news/2023/07/24/kings-college-row-as-white-lecturers-banned-free-tai-chi

31 S. O'Driscoll, 'How major university discriminated against white and Asian candidates', *Newsweek*, Jan 2024; available online: https://www.newsweek.com/university-washington-white-asian-candidates-excluded-employment-interviews-1856321

32 P. Gopal, N. Rollock, and D. Batty, '"Monolithically white places": academics on racism in universities', *Guardian*, Nov 2019; available online: https://www.theguardian.com/education/2019/oct/24/monolithically-white-places-academics-on-racism-in-universities

33 Students for Fair Admissions, 'SFFA's Letters to Yale, Princeton and Duke questioning compliance with SFFA v. Harvard', Sept 2024; available online: https://studentsforfairadmissions.org/students-for-fair-admissions-sends-letters-to-yale-princeton-and-duke-questioning-compliance-with-sffa-v-harvard

34 L. Duggan, 'Universities are still exploiting affirmative action loopholes', *UnHerd*, Jan 2024; available online: https://unherd.com/newsroom/affirmative-action-whats-next-supreme-court

35 'Is DEI causing the "Crisis of free speech" on campus?', Heterodox Academy, Dec 2023; available online: https://heterodoxacademy.org/blog/is-dei-causing-the-crisis-of-free-speech-on-campus

36 T. Slater, 'Beware the university campus microaggression monitors', *Spectator*, Sep 2022, available online: https://www.spectator.co.uk/article/beware-the-university-campus-microaggression-monitors

37 L. Krauss, 'How "diversity" turned tyrannical', *Wall Street Journal*, Oct 2021; available online: https://www.wsj.com/

articles/diversity-tyrannical-equity-inclusion-college-
marginalized-race-11634739677

38   I. X. Kendi, *How to Be an Antiracist* (One World, 2019).

39   M. Goodwin, *Values, Voice and Virtue: The new British
     politics* (Random House, 2023); Ipsos, 'Race is no barrier to
     "being British"', May 2002, available online: https://www.
     ipsos.com/en-uk/race-no-barrier-being-british

40   S. Bunbury, D. Husbands and D. Anand, 'How to be an
     anti-racist ally on the university campus', *Times Higher
     Education*, May 2023; available online: https://www.
     timeshighereducation.com/campus/how-be-antiracist-
     ally-university-campus

41   Advance HE, 'Tackling racism on campus: Raising
     awareness and creating the conditions for confident
     conversations', Feb 2023; available online: https://www.
     advance-he.ac.uk/equality-charters

42   N. Riaz and K. Mohammed, Steering Group Members,
     Advance HE, Morton Ward, and Scottish Funding
     Council, 'Tackling racism on campus assets', Advance HE,
     2019; available online: https://s3.eu-west-2.amazonaws.com/
     assets.creode.advancehe-document-manager/documents/
     advance-he/Tackling%20Racism%20on%20Campus%20
     Assets%20Utilisation%20Guide_1616057561.pdf

43   P. Devine and T. Ash, 'Diversity Training Goals, Limitations,
     and Promise: A Review of the Multidisciplinary literature',
     Annual Review of Psychology, 73(1), 403–429, 2021;
     available online: https://www.annualreviews.org/content/
     journals/10.1146/annurev-psych-060221-122215

44   H. Pluckrose and J. A. Lindsay, *Cynical Theories: How
     activist scholarship made everything about race, gender,*

and identity – and why this harms everybody (Pitchstone
Publishing, 2020), pp.77–8.

45 R. Hewitt, 'New report calls for the decolonisation of
universities in order address a "silent crisis"', HEPI, July
2022; available online: https://www.hepi.ac.uk/2020/07/23/
new-report-calls-for-decolonisation-of-universities-in-
order-address-the-silent-crisis-in-universities

46 R. Norrie, 'Free speech and decolonisation in British
universities', Civitas, 2022; available online: https://civitas.
org.uk/content/files/Free-Speech-Decolonisation-and-
British-Universities-FINAL.pdf

47 D. Stokes, 'Decolonisation is a welcome contribution, but
must not be enforced', HEPI, Mar 2021; available online:
https://www.hepi.ac.uk/2021/03/18/doug-stokes-the-white-
paper-is-vital-for-the-defence-of-academic-freedom

48 Edskids, 'The QAA tells academics to decolonise Classics
and Maths', Committee for Academic Freedom, July
2024; available online: https://afcomm.org.uk/2024/07/16/
the-qaa-tells-academics-to-decolonise-classics-and-maths

49 Cited in Edskids, 'The QAA tells academics to decolonise
Classics and Maths'

50 Universities UK, *Tackling Racial Harassment in
Higher Education*, 2020; available online: https://www.
universitiesuk.ac.uk/what-we-do/policy-and-research/
publications/tackling-racial-harassment-higher

51 D. Stokes, 'The campus grievance industry', *The Critic*,
Sept 2020; available online: https://thecritic.co.uk/issues/
september-2020/the-campus-grievance-industry

52 C. Rufo, 'D.E.I. programs are getting in the way of liberal
education', *New York Times*, July 2023; available online:

https://www.nytimes.com/2023/07/27/opinion/christopher-
rufo-diversity-desantis-florida-university.html

CHAPTER 5: SOLUTIONS

1   A. Sullivan, 'We all live on campus now', *Intelligencer*,
    Feb 2018; available online: https://nymag.com/
    intelligencer/2018/02/we-all-live-on-campus-now.html

2   J. Rauch, *The Constitution of Knowledge: A defense of truth*
    (Brookings Institution Press, 2021).

3   'A letter on justice and open debate', *Harper's Magazine*,
    Aug 2020; available online: https://harpers.org/
    a-letter-on-justice-and-open-debate

4   C. Turner, 'Government faces High Court showdown with
    its free speech tsar', *Telegraph*, Sept 2024; available online:
    https://www.telegraph.co.uk/politics/2024/09/07/free-speech-
    laws-act-tsar-repeal-universities-cancel-ahmed

5   C. Turner, 'Government dropped free speech law after
    universities feared for China interests', *Telegraph*,
    Aug 2024; available online: https://www.telegraph.co.uk/
    politics/2024/08/24/british-universities-lobbied-drop-free-
    speech

6   Turner, 'Government dropped free speech law'.

7   E. Gretzinger, M. Hicks, C. Dutton and J. Smith,
    'Tracking higher ed's dismantling of DEI',
    Chronicle of Higher Education, Nov 2024; available
    online: https://www.chronicle.com/article/
    tracking-higher-eds-dismantling-of-dei

ACKNOWLEDGEMENTS

I would like to thank the following people who, in different ways, helped me during my academic career though who may not agree with everything that I have written in this book. They are: Professors Roger Eatwell, Eric Kaufmann, Harold Clarke, Paul White-ley, David Cutts, Philip Cowley, Paul Heywood, Peter John, Richard Whitman, Doug Stokes, Aleksandra Cichocka, and Caitlin Milazzo. I would also like to thank Charlie Brotherstone and Henry Vines. I would especially like to thank my family.